D1712325

PEOPLE IN PAIN

PEOPLE IN PAIN

A Guide to Pastoral Care

By

JAMES A. VANDERPOOL, Ph.D.

Clinical Director
District of Columbia Government Rehabilitation Center for Alcoholics
Occoquan, Virginia
Diplomate
American Board of Professional Psychologists

CHARLES C THOMAS • PUBLISHER
Springfield · Illinois · U.S.A.

Published and Distributed Throughout the World by

CHARLES C THOMAS ● PUBLISHER

Bannerstone House

301-327 East Lawrence Avenue, Springfield, Illinois, U.S.A.

© *1979, by* CHARLES C THOMAS ● PUBLISHER

ISBN 0-398-03846-5

Library of Congress Catalog Card Number: 78-13045

With THOMAS BOOKS *careful attention is given to all details of*
manufacturing and design. It is the Publisher's desire to present books that
are satisfactory as to their physical qualities and artistic possibilities and
appropriate for their particular use. THOMAS BOOKS *will be true to those*
laws of quality that assure a good name and good will.

Printed in the United States of America
V-R-2

Library of Congress Cataloging in Publication Data

Vanderpool, James A
 People in pain.

 Bibliography: p. 179
 Includes index.
 1. Pastoral counseling. 2. Church work with
the mentally ill. I. Title.
BV4012.2.V27   253.5   78-13045
ISBN 0-398-03846-5

PREFACE

THE twentieth century has produced an increasingly complex society in which the rate of change expands at a shocking pace. We are all familiar with examples of the great gap between man's advancement with machines and man's advancement in helping the suffering. Our institutions are already overburdened with those seeking help for physical and mental afflictions. In addition, the mental health movement has brought increased sympathy and understanding for those who are suffering or are in pain because their behavior is contrary to what is considered normal in a given society.

Atypical behavior may create pain because of self-incrimination, social alienation, isolation, and guilt when such behavior is contrasted with the norms and mores of a culture or social environment. In the present context, therefore, *people in pain* are defined as those who are suffering from mental or emotional distress caused by their behavior, which is viewed either by themselves or others as outside the mainstream of the society. Their pain is real. It may be the result of atypical and bizarre thinking, unwelcomed and painful emotions and feelings, an addiction, antisocial acting-out behavior, or a combination of any and all of these elements.

The pain may be felt also by those who are close to the individual who exhibits the atypical behavior. Thus, counseling may include not only care for an individual but also for significant others, such as family members and friends.

Our modern world has not only increased the number of problems in these areas; but also because of improved communications, we are increasingly more aware of the magnitude of the suffering. When one looks at the great demand for human helping services, compared to the availability of professional help, the need is staggering. The gap must be filled by educating key members of the public, regardless of their backgrounds, to provide help. A missionary in the Philippines, a nursing sister in a hospital, an ordained minister, a priest, or a rabbi may be called on to serve as the counselor for a person in pain or for his or her loved ones. This may be due to the fact that no professionally trained therapists, such as psychologists or psychiatrists, are available, because the professional cannot be consulted for lack of funds, or again, for such personal reasons as the individual does not wish to seek help other than that of the pastoral counselor. The pastoral counselor can help these people in pain by fulfilling a general role of educator and the special role of a counseling pastor, particularly in guilt and values clarification.

This book is a guide to pastoral care for these people in pain. Although readers may come from a variety of backgrounds, it is assumed that they share in common the desire to help those individuals who have problems involving thinking, feelings, and actions that are atypical or considered abnormal in a given social environment.

The pastoral counselor is in a unique position to help people in pain. Often, it is only to him to whom the distressed person turns. In many cases, the pastoral counselor is consulted before any other help is sought. Often, the counselor is in a position to help bring a sense of perspective to the individual's assessment of his crisis, because the person in pain is suffering concurrently from a sense of isolation and turns to the pastoral counselor for consolation and assistance. Thus, the counselor may at the outset break this sense of isolation by reassuring the client that he is not alone and is not the only human being with a particular problem. This in itself may be therapeutically significant and create an atmosphere conducive to counseling.

It is assumed that the person in pain is reaching out in the midst of an intense personal dilemma, if only because of his or her own distorted perceptions. It is assumed that the reader as a pastoral counselor recognizes the need not only to help free the client from a sense of isolation but also to assist the individual in a twofold manner: (1) as an educator or a dispenser of secular and general knowledge and (2) in the special role of a counselor, particularly in matters related to guilt and values.

This book is designed to aid pastoral counselors in fulfilling the role of a general counselor of individuals with atypical behavior problems. It does not intend, however, to presume to teach or recommend that anyone become an amateur psychiatrist or play professional psychologist. On the contrary, the reader is cautioned against pretending or assuming these professional roles. Nonetheless, this does not mean that there is not a great deal non- or paraprofessional counselors, as well as trained pastoral counselors, can do to help a person and assist the individual in changing or altering atypical and maladaptive behavior. It is the absence of professional clinicians and medical personnel that makes the role of pastoral counselor doubly important, as he or she is an educator and counselor to many people in pain.

My earlier book, *Person to Person: A Handbook for Pastoral Counseling*, discussed guidance for different ages and stages of human development. This book treats, instead, counseling individuals, regardless of age, whose behavior is considered atypical for a given society.

General procedures for counseling disturbed persons are presented. The major portion of the book is case studies. Cases are examined, using the same basic sequence in the presentation: (1) presentation of the case; (2) developing procedures for approaching and helping the person with the atypical behavior; (3) a summary of significant activities in the actual counseling relationship, with particular attention to matters involving guilt and values; and (4) a report of results and evaluation.

Throughout the book, it is emphasized that, for convenience, human behavior may be classified arbitrarily as a particular type of behavior. However, humans cannot be classified; human beings cannot be diagnosed, except as persons to be loved and respected. Only behavior can be considered atypical, abnormal, or maladaptive.

It is to be noted that the personal pronoun *I* represents the counselor in the case presentations. The first person narrator in many of the cases is not me but is some other professional counselor or individual in a helping profession. Further, the cases have been altered to assure anonymity of both the counselor and client and the details changed to make points clear in the counseling process.

On my desk, I have one of my favorite prayers, which I recommend to all who wish to be a pastoral counselor.

J.A.V.

Lord, make me an instrument of your peace
Where there is hatred — let me sow love.
Where there is injury — pardon.
Where there is doubt — faith.
Where there is despair — hope.
Where there is darkness — light.
Where there is sadness — joy.

O Divine Master, grant that I may not so much seek
To be consoled — as to console,
To be understood — as to understand,
To be loved — as to love,
                                    for
It is in giving — that we receive,
It is in pardoning — that we are pardoned,
It is in dying — that we are born to eternal life.

St. Francis of Assisi

ACKNOWLEDGMENTS

I AM grateful to my devoted friend and secretary, Mrs. George (Ruby) Heflin, for typing and proofreading the original manuscript and its revisions; Rosalie Tabler, for doing some of the typing; Larry H. Cash for proofreading; and Dolores F. Wright, Director, Department of Drug and Alcohol Concerns, Board of Church and Society of the United Methodist Church, for material on drugs and drug abuse.

I wish to thank, in a special way, Lillian Brownfield, R.N., Dennis M. Waszak, S.D.S., and many other counselors for contributing case studies.

I am particularly grateful to my personal friend and professional counseling colleague, John Porter, for serving as critic and consultant.

This guide is especially dedicated to my fellow professional pastoral counselors. Ours is a glorious and sacred vocation. It is precisely because there are so few of us that this attempt is made to assist others in the helping professions, not only to understand our vocation, but also to share in our work insofar as they are competent when we are not available.

Finally, I am grateful not only to the hundreds who have allowed me to be their counselor, but also to those teachers and friends to whom I have turned when in pain.

J.A.V.

CONTENTS

  9. CASE STUDIES OF ATYPICAL ACTING OUT AND
       ANTISOCIAL BEHAVIOR 114
 10. CASE STUDIES OF ALCOHOL DEPENDENCY,
       SOCIOPATHOLOGY, AND DRUG ADDICTION 124

PART V
OTHER PERSONS IN PAIN

 11. CASE STUDIES INVOLVING HUMAN SEXUALITY 143

PART VI
CONCLUSION

 12. THE ROLE OF THE PASTORAL COUNSELOR 173

     Bibliography 179
     Index 187

PEOPLE IN PAIN

Part I
Introduction

CHAPTER 1

COUNSELING PROCEDURES

HUMAN BEINGS AND HUMAN BEHAVIOR

THERE is no such thing as a normal person. There are individuals who have made a relatively good adjustment to themselves, to others, and to their society. Perhaps these are the only normal individuals — that is, those who more or less conform to a norm in a given society.

Just as there are no normal persons, there are no abnormal persons: They do not exist. There are individuals, however, whose behavior does not conform in some way with the norms of a given society. Their behavior is *atypical*. This atypical behavior may be (1) in thinking, (2) in feeling, (3) in actions, or (4) in any combination of these three. Atypical behavior often causes problems and pain for the person, his associates, his society, or all three.

In dealing with individuals whose behavior does not conform to the norms of a given society, there is too often the tendency to confuse the person with the behavior and label the person *abnormal*. This is unfortunate and can have a profound effect on an individual. There is, for example, no such person as a "schizophrenic," an "alcoholic" or a "neurotic"; instead, there are fallible human beings whose atypical behavior has caused the persons to be labeled *abnormal*, rather than the behavior being labeled *atypical*. This is regrettable, for it confuses the person with the problem behavior. It is more correct, therefore, to speak of a person whose thinking behavior is schizophrenic, a fallible human being who has an alcohol problem, or a person who feels neurotically anxious.

It is important for the pastoral counselor to keep in mind that in all cases he or she is dealing with fallible human beings who are normal in the sense that they are human beings whose behavior, on the other hand, may be atypical or contrary to the norm of a given society. This behavior in turn may create a problem and possibly pain for the individual and his or her friends, loved ones, and society.

ATYPICAL BEHAVIOR, PROBLEMS, AND PERSONS

When a person whose behavior is atypical for his society comes for counseling, a counselor must initially consider three things: (1) the atypical behavior, (2) the underlying problems, and (3) the person as a potential client.

1. It is not important for the pastoral counselor to concentrate on the atypical behavior of a client. Irrational thinking, unwanted emotions, anxiety, and drunkenness, etc., are easy to recognize. Often, these are only symptoms of deeper problems.

2. Ordinarily, the pastoral counselor is not able to handle possible underlying causes or deeper problems evoking the atypical behavior. The possible frustrations, conflicts, or pressures antecedent to the behavior, in most cases, is not within the competence of the counselor to handle. Except in those cases where the basic problem involves guilt or values, treatment of any underlying problems should be left to other professionals, such as doctors, psychiatrists, or psychologists.

3. The pastoral counselor's main concern is, existentially, the person here and now who, for whatever reason, suffers or causes others to suffer because of atypical behavior. The counselor helps the individual first, and then as far as possible, aids him or her in avoiding atypical behavior and substituting adaptive for maladaptive behavior.

COUNSELING PROCEDURES

There are four general counseling procedures to be followed when dealing with a person whose behavior is atypical: (1) *a preliminary assessment* of the person as a potential client, the atypical behavior, the competency of the counselor to handle the person, and the desirability of establishing a counseling relationship; (2) deciding, after the preliminary assessment, upon an appropriate *approach to the person*; (3) developing an *approach to the atypical behavior* and, in a few cases, an approach to the underlying problem; and (4) *pastoral counseling.*

PROCEDURE 1. THE PRELIMINARY ASSESSMENT

The first procedure involves a preliminary assessment of the person as a potential client and the competency of the counselor. After a person has come to a pastoral counselor the counselor should ask him- or herself certain questions before accepting the client:

1. Do I want the client? Does the client want me to be his counselor?
2. Should the patient have a physical examination or other examination before any attempt at counseling is initiated?
3. Is the atypical behavior in the area of thinking, feeling, acting out, or any combination of these three? Do I understand such behavior well enough to be able to help the client?
4. Am I competent to handle the person? To what degree am I competent? Is the underlying problem an appropriate one for me to handle? Does it involve guilt or values? To what degree am I competent to help the client eliminate the atypical behavior?
5. What are the goals of a counseling relationship from my point of view and from the point of view of the client? Are the goals realistic and attainable?
6. Is there guilt involved? Is it irrational or rational guilt or a combination of both? What can I do to help the client dissipate and overcome his guilt feelings?
7. Does the client want me to help him assess his moral and spiritual value systems in terms of creativity and their energizing and sustaining qualities? Does he need to change his value system? If so, can I help it? Does he need me to help him reinforce his present value system? Are our two value systems so antithetical that I am unable to be objective? Can I accept the potential client's value system even if it is at variance with mine?
8. Most important and ultimately, the critical question is:

Regardless of the atypical behavior, *will I* as a counselor be able to influence in a positive way the *thinking* of the client so that he can change his behavior?

PROCEDURE 2. APPROACH TO THE PERSON

If it is determined that the counselor is at least to some degree competent to help the client and both desire to enter a counseling relationship, the next step is to determine an appropriate approach to the person. Three matters should be considered: empathic understanding, attitude toward the client and counseling techniques.

Empathic Understanding

At the outset, the counselor must ask himself certain questions:

1. Will I as a counselor be able to listen empathetically to the client? That is, will I be able to listen to both the verbal and nonverbal communications of the client? Will I be able to hear what the client feels as well as listen to what is said?
2. Will I be able to convey to the client that he or she is understood and is accepted without censure, no matter what is discussed?
3. Will the client feel safe and understood? Will I be able to convey to him that everything discussed in the counseling sessions is privileged and confidential?

Without empathic understanding on the part of the pastoral counselor, little if anything can be accomplished. If the counselor feels he cannot achieve empathy within a reasonable time, he should disqualify himself.

Attitude Toward the Client

Next, the counselor must ask him- or herself what attitude he or she should take in dealing with the client. Shall I be authoritative or supportive? Should I use a directive or a nondirective approach? Should I use some other approach to the client, such as simply listening as a friend, rather than as a counselor?

Approaches to clients vary. If a counselor listens to the client and has some understanding of the client's problem and behavior, it is seldom difficult to determine the proper attitude and approach to the client.

A young girl was brought to a counselor because she was wetting the bed each night. When the mother of the girl brought her to the counselor, it was obvious from the beginning that she was shy and felt very insecure. In this case, the counselor correctly adopted a supportive approach to the child. On the other hand, a teenage boy was brought to a counselor. The young man had been drinking excessively and smoking pot and had been disruptive in his behavior both at home and at school. It was necessary, at least at first, for the counselor to use an authoritative and direct approach.

A woman who was very nervous and upset came to a counselor. In this case, it was helpful to use a nondirective approach and to allow the woman to talk freely with little or no interruption.

A man came to a counselor claiming that he was God. The counselor did not argue with the man but decided he could do nothing more than to listen as a friend might do, since counseling, as such, seemed impossible. He did not laugh or make fun of the man; the counselor simply listened, empathetically, as the client described his world as he perceived it.

In general, a dictatorial approach should not be used. At all times, the counselor should avoid attempts to impose his standards and his value systems on the client. At no time should the counselor "play God," for he too is a fallible human being and can make mistakes even in the counseling relationship.

Counseling Techniques

The technique used in counseling depends on the training that the counselor has received. When a pastor has had a minimum of counseling training, *reality counseling techniques* may be easily learned.

Reality counseling or *reality therapy* is a relatively simple technique. It is, essentially, listening empathically while the client describes him- or herself and his or her problems, behavior, family background, present living situation, occupation, interests, and likes and dislikes, etc. The client is allowed to talk about *his real world as he perceives it.* Whether the facts are accurately presented is not important. Often, the discrepancy of the world as the client perceives it and the world about the client as it really is can give the counselor clues to possible problems that exist for the client.

After the counselor has permitted the client to speak about his world and possibly ventilate some of his feelings and release some of his tension, the counselor can then proceed to discuss the client's world with him. This is done in the hope that the client may see the discrepancy between his and the real world and then may adopt more adaptive behavior to substitute for his atypical behavior.

In using reality techniques, the counselor should be careful to avoid certain pitfalls: (1) talking too much and not listening to both the verbal and nonverbal communication of the client ; (2) asking questions, particularly closed-ended questions requiring a yes or no answer; (3) jumping to conclusions; (4) giving advice; (5) terminating the counseling too soon or prolonging it beyond the time needed to achieve the counseling goals; and (6) attempting to impose upon the client the counselor's own standards, values, and point of view. Above all, the counselor must listen and avoid holding rigidly to predetermined goals to be achieved in a particular session. An effective counselor determines before each session, goals to be accomplished. However, he must not discourage the client from talking freely. Often, he or she may need to alter the session's goals because of what the client says, the client's mood, and the existential needs of the client at the time.

PROCEDURE 3. APPROACH TO PROBLEMS
AND ATYPICAL BEHAVIOR

Counselors know there are many deep-seated problems that cause or occasion atypical behavior. Again, most pastoral counselors are not competent to handle the underlying problems that have led to the atypical behavior, unless these problems are specifically in the areas of guilt and value clarification. The counselor can guide the client in substituting adaptive behavior for the atypical or maladaptive behavior. In this role, he or she serves as a secular educator and/or counselor.

Two approaches to help the client substitute adaptive behavior for maladaptive or atypical behavior are recommended: (1) a type of *crisis intervention* as a holistic approach to the person and his behavior and (2) the use of certain principles and techniques of *rational behavior therapy* (RBT) to deal with specific problem areas, such as unwanted or undesirable emotions.

Crisis Intervention

In dealing with the individual as a unique person, the counselor may seek to explore with the client possible alternative behavior more in conformity to his or her society than the behavior that is a source of concern. The pastoral counselor does not attempt to alter personality development, treat mental illness, or handle the underlying causes of anxious or neurotic behavior; he or she can assist many clients in finding adaptive alternatives to maladaptive behavior. The philosophy of so-called crisis intervention is the belief that, in nearly every case, alternative and more rewarding or satisfactory behavior can be found for nonrewarding or atypical behavior. Once having recognized the behavior, the pastoral counselor is able, in many cases, to suggest alternatives to the atypical behavior. For example to one who drinks excessively when he gets angry, adaptive means to handle stresses, strains, anxiety, disappointments, and unwanted emotions rather than drinking (which, in most cases, simply aggravates the problem), can be found. Exercise, rewarding hobbies, and association with friends or with others who have had similar problems, such as those in Alcoholics Anonymous (AA) can be used as adaptive behavior. All these are alternatives to the maladaptive drinking behavior; there are many more.

Crisis intervention is recommended for the pastoral counselor, since medical or similar professional knowledge is not necessary in employing the technique. A more detailed discussion of its use by pastoral counselors may be found in Glenn E. Whitlock's *Preventive Psychology and the Church* (Philadelphia, Westminister Press, 1973).

Principles and Techniques of Rational Behavior Therapy

No counselor, professional, or paraprofessional can deal with a complex group of problems of a person at one time. One of the mistakes made by many counselors is the attempt to heal the whole person and to solve all the person's problems at once. It is essential to separate problem behavior into individual components and to deal with each component separately.

It was useless to attempt to deal with a general behavior pattern of a woman who became angry and abusive in many and varied situations. It was essential that the counselor helped her select a specific event at a specific time that caused her anger and work with this event and the irrational emotion that followed. In this way, it was possible for the counselor to teach her how she could substitute rational thinking for the irrational thinking that preceded and produced the unwanted emotion of anger. Thus, these unwanted emotions and the maladaptive behavior that followed from her feelings of anger were avoided.

A young seminarian came to a pastoral counselor and was much concerned because he was drinking too much and feared he had a problem with alcohol. In addition, he was concerned about his homosexual tendencies and the fact that another seminarian he desired had rejected him. Finally, he was almost ready for ordination and he was not sure of his vocation. It would have been impossible for both the client and counselor to solve all these problems at one time. Instead, it was necessary for the counselor to have the client separate these problem areas and work on them one at a time. After the first session, the client was instructed to concentrate on the drinking problem and to decide if, indeed, he had a problem of chronic alcoholism. After this matter was settled, the question of his homosexual tendencies was explored and assistance was given the client in forming a certain conscience about them; that is, he was guided in deciding what he considered to be right and wrong in these matters. Next, the matter of his religious vocation was considered, and, finally with the use of rational behavior therapy, the unwanted emotions of anger and depression regarding his fellow seminarian's rejection were dissipated.

Increasingly, counselors are using rational behavior therapy or a modified form of this counseling and therapeutic technique. Increasingly more pastoral counselors are learning this technique and teaching it to their clients so that they can become their own counselors and therapists. It is based upon the empirically demonstrated postulants that *what one thinks determines what one feels* and *what one feels and thinks determines one's actions*, including atypical behavior. It follows that if a person changes his or her thinking, that person can alter or change his or her feelings and actions. This does not deny the converse, that actions influence feelings and these influence what one thinks. However, in counseling, the effect of changes in thinking that affect feelings and actions are relatively more important.

One of the basic assumptions of rational behavior therapy and counseling is that, to the degree one can influence the thinking of another, he can influence the individual's behavior. That is, when a counselor influences, positively, the thinking of a client regardless of the atypical behavior, the counselor assists the client in overcoming or correcting the atypical behavior. Further, when a pastoral counselor influences, positively, a client's thinking in matters related to guilt and values, he is fulfilling his unique role as a pastoral counselor. "For as a man thinketh in his heart, so is he." (Prov. 23:7)

PROCEDURE 4. PASTORAL COUNSELING

The special and specific role of the pastoral counselor is to deal with problems involving guilt or values or both. Indirectly but incidentally, the counselor may help a client with other problems. However, at all times, the pastoral counselor should be aware of and concentrate on problems of guilt and values, which may have some bearing or influence on the atypical behavior.

Guilt:

A pastoral counselor must realize that one of his most important and unique functions is to aid a client in all matters that have to do with guilt and any culpability a client may feel for any and all actions. He must help a client to distinguish between "irrational" or emotional guilt and "rational" or moral guilt. He must enable a client to recognize irrational or emotional guilt arising ordinarily because of an individual's likes and dislikes. This arousal is due to spontaneous, emotional, and irrational responses to stimuli. These are "animal" emotional responses, not under the control of reason and, therefore, they have no moral content. The counselor should guide the client in recognizing these irrational responses to stimuli and help the client eliminate guilt feelings that may exist because of these responses.

On the other hand, rational or moral guilt is based upon the violations by an individual of his own rational value systems. In cases involving actual moral guilt, the counselor should help the client find, based on his or her value system, appropriate and adequate means for alleviation of the guilt, such as confession, prayer, restitution, and apologies.

Values

Concerning values, the pastoral counselor should assist the client in determining what his or her value system is; that is, what his or her subjective standards for belief and conduct are. Next, the counselor should help the client evaluate these value systems in his or her own terms, deciding whether or not they are sustaining, creative, and energizing. If any or all three characteristics of meaningful values are missing, the counselor should assist the client in clarifying or developing new value systems. Usually, this, in turn involves examination of the client's theology and religious beliefs before meaningful value systems may be formulated.

Elimination of guilt and the development of meaningful value systems can contribute to changes in client behaviors. In many instances, it facilitates the elimination of atypical behavior. This special role of the pastoral counselor in the areas of guilt and values usually cannot be fulfilled by other professionals.

CONCLUSION

Procedures for dealing as a pastoral counselor with persons whose behavior in a given society is considered atypical has been outlined. It comprises four sections: (1) *A preliminary assessment* includes an evaluation of the client, the problem, the atypical behavior, and the competence of the counselor; (2) *an approach to the person* is developed; (3) *the approach to problems and atypical behavior* of the client are determined; and (4) *pastoral counseling*, dealing with guilt and values, is treated as the most important function.

In Chapter 2 it is shown that these procedures form an integral part in the four-part case studies including case presentation, procedures, counseling and discussion, and evaluation and results.

Only a brief summary of the nature and duties of the pastor as counselor has been given. Guilt, values, and value systems have only been noted and not discussed in detail. For a more complete treatment of these, one may refer to my earlier book *Person to Person: A Handbook for Pastoral Counseling* (New York, Doubleday & Co., 1977).

CHAPTER 2

A METHOD FOR THE CASE STUDY
OF ATYPICAL BEHAVIOR

THE cases of atypical behavior presented in
the next sections are actual cases. Names, however, and any
detail that might reveal the identity of the individual have been
changed. Sometimes, the cases are altered slightly to illustrate
or emphasize a point. None of the cases are presented as models
but rather as illustrations of the use of the procedures presented earlier. They will assist counselors in developing their
own procedures for dealing with diverse individuals with different types and kinds of atypical behavior.

The cases are divided into those involving *atypical thinking,*
atypical feeling, and, *atypical acting-out.* This division is, ad-
mittedly, arbitrary and somewhat artificial, since it is the belief
of this author that most, if not all, atypical behavior is, ultimately, a matter of *what one thinks.* The division into the three
classes of cases was made solely on the basis of the primary
external manifestations or symptoms of the atypical behavior.

Professionals and many nonprofessionals will recognize in
the section dealing with cases of *atypical thinking* cases that are
categorized as "mental retardation," "brain damage," "psy-
chosis." Similarly, some call the cases treated as *atypical feeling*
"manic," "depressive," or "neurotic." Finally, cases involving
atypical acting out are often labeled "personality disorders" or
"sociopathology," as well as cases involving alcohol or drug
dependency. As indicated earlier, labels and diagnosis should
be avoided, particularly by the pastoral counselor, since there is
the general tendency to confuse a person with his or her behavior. In no way does this assist the person; it may do a great
deal of harm. The pastoral counselor should avoid attempts at
diagnosis or classification. He or she should remember, at all

16

times, his responsibility to help any person in pain, regardless of the form or kind of atypical behavior associated with the individual.

Cases that involve actual physical disorders are not treated. Earlier, it was recommended that a pastoral counselor consider at all time the possibility that a potential client should be referred to a physician or, at least, undergo a physical examination before the counseling relationship begins. Often, the counselor finds that he can cooperate with a physician, which is to the advantage of the client; many times, it is wise to defer counseling until after physical treatment or a person is medically cleared for treatment.

Cases that involve *transient* conditions associated with different stages and ages in the chronological growth of an individual, such as childhood, adolescence, middlescence, and old age, also are not discussed.

The cases are presented in the following manner:

Case Presentation

A short history of the case, including dialogue between the counselor and client and other material that may seem relevant in dealing with the person and his or her problem, is included in this section. For simplification, the material in each case is presented as if it were obtained in one session, while, in reality, many sessions may have been involved.

Procedures

Following the case presentation are the procedures discussed in Chapter 1:

1. The preliminary assessment
2. Approach to the person
3. Approach to problems and atypical behavior
4. Pastoral counseling

A pastoral counselor should use any counseling technique he feels is appropriate or use various techniques for different cases or differing approaches at different sessions with a single client. Being eclectic permits the counselor to freely employ whatever techniques he or she wishes or feels comfortable in using. As a generalization — which has many exceptions — eclectic counselors tend to use reality counseling techniques when dealing with individuals whose cases involve atypical thinking. Nondirective and rational behavior techniques are used for those whose problems involve atypical feelings, and more authoritative and reality techniques are employed when a person's acting-out behavior is atypical. In the last instance, the counselor often serves as educator so that counseling can be done. This is particularly true when the atypical behavior involves alcoholism, drug dependency, or criminal and antisocial behavior.

Counseling and Discussion

The counseling and discussion section is a condensation of the actual counseling sessions, including a discussion of the objectives and goals of the counseling relationship.

No single model can be given for the pastor to use in counseling. However, many counselors have found the following simple model, or a modification of it, helpful in many cases.

1. After the preliminary assessment of the desirability and potential of a counseling relationship, as indicated earlier, approaches are determined by the counselor to the person and to the problems and atypical behavior, insofar as it is appropriate and possible for the counselor to handle.

2. With the client, the counselor explores the client's past to determine possible guilt that may have arisen, particularly as such guilt may have been related to the atypical behavior. The pastor assists the client — no matter how many sessions it takes — in finding ways to alleviate both his or her irrational and rational guilt.

3. The backward look, however, should also be positive, including an assessment of past rewarding goals, values, achievements, and those events, persons, or things that have helped rather than hindered the client's self-actualization and

strengthened his self-esteem, self-confidence, and self-concept.

4. Following the examination of the past, it is most important to consider the present and look to the future to determine realistic goals and values. This may involve exploration of the various value systems of the client and even the individual's theology, philosophy, and religious beliefs. Often, this examination is hard work for both the pastor and the client. However, it is essential with clients when it is possible and to the degree that the client can formulate value systems and determine realistic goals.

5. Finally, the counselor and client may explore together possible alternatives to the atypical maladaptive behavior. They also may discuss the use of more adaptive behavior in handling stress, strains, and anxiety. Through rational behavior therapy or similar methods, it is often possible to find responses to life situations and personal crises resulting from more positive and rational thinking. These replace and thus eliminate atypical behavior that has caused problems and pain for the client.

Evaluation and Results

This section, evaluation and results, is devoted to a brief discussion of the case, a recapitulation of any important points that need emphasizing, and most importantly, the results achieved through the counseling relationship.

Many people have served as counselors in the cases presented: professionals and para- or nonprofessionals; lay people, religious, and clergy; males and females. None of the counselors are identified by name. Instead, the personal pronoun *I* is used to identify the pastoral counselor, regardless of sex, race, training, religion, or personal characteristics.

Part II
Atypical and Bizarre Thinking

CHAPTER 3

ATYPICAL AND BIZARRE THINKING

WORKING with individuals whose primary symptom of atypical behavior is in the area of thinking and the intellect can be frustrating and discouraging for the neophyte pastoral counselor, as it is at times for trained psychiatrists, psychologists, and other mental health professionals. One often asks him- or herself, "How can I help this person? There seems so little that I can do." Realizing that only to the degree that one can change or influence the thinking of a potential client, it is true that in many cases the assistance and counseling that can be done is limited. This is particularly true in cases where the behavior may stem from physical disabilities, impairments, or mental or physical limitations. Yet, even in the seemingly most difficult cases, there is ordinarily something the pastoral counselor can do to help the person or his or her loved ones. Even though all the procedures outlined earlier cannot be followed completely, in nearly every case, positive influence and results can be made by the counselor who (1) is willing to be *available* and (2) is willing to *listen*, empathically and patiently, to the person.

The pastoral counselor should be encouraged by the knowledge that, in recent years, a great deal more can be done with the potential of many who suffer from so-called mental retardation or brain damage than was thought in the past. Further, it is true that individuals who evidence so-called schizophrenic behavior or psychotic thinking at times may become rationally approachable. With patience — and time — a great deal more can be done in many cases than might have seemed possible when counseling first was considered.

It was gratifying to witness what time, patience, and love could do in what many had considered an impossible situation. It came to the attention of certain federal health officials that one of the poor states in the United States was attempting to care without adequate staff or facilities for a large number of mentally retarded children. The children lived in cottages that reminded one of pigsties, rather than the warm home any child deserves. When visited, the children were sitting listlessly on a concrete floor. Many wore only diapers, and many of the diapers smelled from the urine and feces that had gone unattended. The atmosphere was one of gloom and despair.

The federal officials were told these children were "hopeless cases"; they did not agree. They determined to find funds to provide rugs, toys, and beds to make one of the cottages more homelike and to supply funds for clothing and a larger staff. For the staff, they chose not expensive professionals but paraprofessionals who loved children and indicated by their words and actions that they understood what was necessary in terms of time, patience, and expectations. Six months later, local TV stations carried the story of the "miracle" at the childrens' home. It showed happy children playing and smiling. Some children bragged that they could "potty" without any help, and two or three showed how they were learning to tie their own shoes. All this was accomplished by the children's counselors, a multiracial group of men and women, many who had only high school educations.

The pastoral counselor should not be discouraged because he or she recognizes limitations in the help that may be given an individual. In many cases, not only is the counselor able to help the person but may, more importantly, help the family and friends of individuals evidencing atypical thinking behavior, particularly as these intimates may feel guilt or responsible, at least to some degree, for the problem of the loved one.

Special Considerations

In cases when it appears that the primary symptom involves atypical thinking, certain specific matters should be considered as a part of procedure 1., the preliminary assessment. Again, they are important not to make a diagnosis but to assist the pastoral counselor in assessing the feasibility, desirability, and potential results of a counseling relationship. The following questions should be answered:

1. Does the atypical thinking involve an inability to think at the level of the average person in the individual's society?
2. Does it involve bizarre or unusual thinking?
3. Is the problem not one that involves atypical thinking as such but appears so, on the surface, because the individual is illiterate, culturally deprived, uneducated, or now functioning poorly after a head injury, or because of poor health or serious physical handicap?
4. Has the atypical thinking existed for most of the life of the client? Has it been present for a long period of time, or has it resulted after something important or traumatic has occurred, such as the death of a loved one, the birth of a child, or following menopause, or has it simply arisen in old age?
5. In what way can I as a pastoral counselor, not a clinician, influence the thinking of the client so that the atypical behavior can be eliminated or at least minimized?
6. Can I influence, positively, the value system of the individual and help alleviate any guilt that may be felt, or if I cannot help the individual directly in these areas, can I help loved ones of the client who may feel guilt for the condition of the person or need their personal value systems refined or altered in view of the client's behavior?

CHAPTER 4

CASE STUDIES OF ATYPICAL AND BIZARRE THINKING

Edna

Case Presentation

M R. AND MRS. JOHNSON came to see me about their daughter, Edna. They had two other girls, both doing well in high school, and an older son who had left home, married, and started his own mechanic shop. Mrs. Johnson began tearfully and almost hysterically, "What, oh what have Fred and I done to deserve this punishment? Edna is now thirteen and still cannot tie her shoes; a doctor tells us she will never be able to read or write. She is very naughty at home and disrupts the whole family. She gets mad and kicks and scratches the other children. . . . We never have a peaceful moment." Mrs. Johnson stopped and began to sob and look at the floor. Her husband Fred said nothing and simply shrugged his shoulders.

I did not know Edna very well, so that when the Johnsons suggested I come to dinner one evening, I agreed. When I arrived, Edna and I seemed to hit it off very well. She would eye me, then laugh and watch my every move. When we were eating, all were surprised to see her climb in my lap and look at me and giggle. At one point she gave me a big hug and a kiss on the cheek. The whole visit was spoiled, however, by the constant nagging Mrs. Johnson did toward Edna. Every minute or so it was, "Edna, now don't do that — don't do this. . . ."

It was clear at the end of the evening that there was little I could do directly to help Edna improve her thinking processes, but there was a great deal I could do indirectly for Edna, if her parents agreed. It was equally clear that the Johnsons, particularly Mrs. Johnson, could benefit by counseling. They agreed to come to me regularly.

Procedures

1. A preliminary assessment suggested that I needed to not only educate the couple in what they could do for Edna but also to assist them in overcoming the guilt they felt for her condition and to help them reexamine their value systems.

2. I decided to see the couple together and serve both as an educator on what I felt they might do for Edna and as a pastoral counselor to help them to overcome any guilt they might feel and to understand and redefine their values.

3. A type of crisis intervention seemed appropriate for Edna, that is, to help the couple find an alternative life situation for Edna.

4. The guilt to be dissipated and the examination of the value systems of the Johnsons would be more difficult and lengthy, since it would involve not only education but changes in the thinking about values on the part of the couple.

Counseling and Discussion

Mr. and Mrs. Johnson came for several sessions. In regard to Edna, it was pointed out that: (1) Edna was hostile because she was expected to act in a way the Johnsons considered normal but which was impossible for her. (2) It was suggested that Edna might profit and the family find greater peace if she were to be placed in a home for special children where she and her peers could live a normal life according to her abilities and those of the other children. It was pointed out that a great deal more can be done than was thought in the past for mentally handicapped children if attempts are not made to force them to live according to the norms of society in general and they are permitted to live according to their own norms. At first, the Johnsons were not receptive to the idea of sending Edna to the special school. As one said, "What will the neighbors think if we put her in such a home? Some will say we have failed and had to do it."

To aid the Johnsons in overcoming their guilt feelings, the counselor had to show them that Edna probably suffered a birth defect and nothing that they did caused the arrested thinking process. The guilt they felt was therefore irrational and emotional. In no way could it be considered moral or rational guilt, since, to the best of their knowledge, the Johnsons had done nothing knowingly and deliberately to cause the condition. In time, they came to understand. Their tension and anxiety was reduced, and the counseling was then able to proceed.

The most difficult task was to help the Johnsons with their spiritual and moral value system. Several times the counselor had to return to one of the first statements made by Mrs. Johnson "What, oh, what have Fred and I done to deserve this punishment?" and to the statement, "What will the neighbors think? . . . Some will say we have failed." Clearly, their theology was inadequate for mature spiritual and moral value systems. Gradually, the counselor guided the couple to a more adequate value system based, in their case, on not only their lifelong belief in a God but also on the fact no one is perfect and that all people are fallible human beings who are not expected to be God.

Evaluation and Results

Edna was placed in a fine school. She felt no separation anxiety in leaving home. Instead, the Johnsons were told it took a remarkably short time for Edna to adjust to the home, her peers, and the counselors. She had many friends and was well liked. She showed no hostility; on the contrary, she took great pleasure in helping some of the other children. It was a proud day for both Edna and her parents when they visited her one day and she showed them how she had taught Sylvia, her favorite friend, to tie her shoes. "Suffer the little children to come unto me, and forbid them not: for of such is the kingdom of God." (Luke 18:16)

It was not overnight that the Johnsons developed an adequate value system for themselves. However, it was gratifying to both the couple and the counselor that the energy that had been used negatively in their home, causing arguments, disagreements, and problems, was now being directed positively toward developing moral and spiritual values that could help them make the kind of home they desired.

Thomas

Case Presentation

Thomas was a twenty-three-year-old man. He had only a fourth grade education, as he had dropped out of school after failing fifth grade twice. Thomas lived with his much-older sister, Martha. He spent most of his days sitting idly at home, staring at the walls, although, daily and impulsively, he cleaned the kitchen in their home.

Martha was an unselfish woman who worked in a factory, doing piecework. Except for church attendance, Martha spent the balance of her time taking care of Thomas. Before she came for counseling, it had become evident to the counselor and others that she was tired, haggard, and unhappy most of the time.

Martha was not one to complain. However, one day she came to me and asked, "Isn't there something more I can do for Tom than I am doing to make his life happier? Poor boy, he sits alone at home day in and day out. He's good — he does everything he thinks he can to help me, especially in the kitchen. Honestly, though, I feel guilty that I am not helping him more. Can you help me?" I assured her I would welcome seeing both of them.

Procedures

A preliminary assessment indicated that I would enjoy working with Martha and with Thomas as well. I planned to see each of them separately at first and then together later. A reality technique seemed to be advisable to determine whether there were things that could be done to improve both their lives. Further, it was clear that in the counseling it would be important to help Martha overcome any guilt she might feel "for not helping him more." Further, it would be necessary to help each develop value systems that could be creative, energizing, and sustaining. It was clear that Tom's value system might be much simpler than Martha's, but a system nonetheless could be developed.

Counseling and Discussion

Thomas was a pleasant young man, shy, and inhibited, who, during the first sessions, kept his head down and stared at the floor. Gradually, however, as the sessions continued, he seemed to feel safer and less frightened. It was not long until he was looking at me during the sessions without fear or restraint.

I proceeded as follows: (1) As a secular counselor, I tried to understand what skills or abilities Thomas might possess. Not many were apparent, at first. Soon, however, it was clear that he liked to work around food and the kitchen, that is why he often helped Martha with the dishes and cleaned the kitchen. As he said, "I like to do things in the kitchen because I love Martha and want to help — and — also — I can't explain it, but it's fun in the kitchen." (2) He felt no guilt for his condition; therefore, nothing had to be attempted in this area. However, (3) he needed a value system. It turned out to be a simple one: to be nice to Martha, to help her in any way he could, to keep his room tidy and himself clean, to go to church and to say his prayers every night, and to get a job.

Counseling Martha was a pleasure. It was necessary to help her to overcome her guilt feelings that she was not "helping him more." It was necessary to show her that she could not do everything she would like for those she loved; further, that other humans, such as Thomas, have limitations in what they can receive. In time, it was accepted by Martha that her value system needed more existential elements; that she should not look back on what she felt she had failed to do or look too much into the future in what she would wish to attain. She was to look at "now" and do what she should first for herself today, then for her loved ones such as Thomas, and in her own way show her daily love of God.

Evaluation and Results

It was suggested to both Thomas and Martha that there were jobs that Thomas could do that would not only keep him busy but also would bring some money — however little — that would help in the running of the house. Because of his interest in kitchen work, a job was found for Tom in a restaurant near his home, within walking distance. He became an excellent worker and loved his job. The last time I was in the restaurant, he spoke with pride as he showed me "his" spotless kitchen. At church, too, on Sunday Martha looked less tense. She no longer sat alone in the pew. Thomas had arranged to be off and with her on Sundays. "Inasmuch as you have done it unto one of the least of these my brother you have done it unto me." (Matt. 25:40)

Henry

As a newly ordained priest and being somewhat apprehensive, I was assigned to visit the state mental hospital once a week. While discussing my role with a more experienced chaplain, he informed me that the patients I would see were diagnosed as suffering from thinking disorders called *schizophrenia*. Often, these patients would hear voices or see persons or things that were not real or actually existed; others would have delusions of being God, the devil, an animal, a rock, or some human or ethereal being. Some could become hostile, aggressive, or suspicious if one challenged their delusions. The chaplain indicated that most of these patients were on medication that often made it possible, at one time or another, to communicate rationally with them. These were the moments for which a pastoral counselor must patiently wait. Even then, over a long period of time, they might occur rarely and unpredictably.

It was suggested by the older chaplain that the best approach in counseling would be for me to listen without censure or criticism, even though I might not believe in much that was delusionally claimed, as true. This was my attitude and approach to Henry.

Henry was a young Irishman of about thirty years of age who had been institutionalized for four years. Little counseling progress had been made with Henry because he was hostile and suspicious of those who attempted to approach him. Henry suffered from delusions of persecution, and when challenged, he had become dangerous to his family and friends. Therefore, he was committed.

I felt somewhat uneasy when I met Henry. He eyed me suspiciously and said little. I said hello and tried to be as pleasant as I could be under the circumstances. This continued for three visits. I was surprised on my fourth visit to be informed that Henry wanted to see me. For the first time, he indicated he wanted to talk. In a confidential whisper, he informed me that he was, secretly, a member of the FBI and that foreign agents were out to get him. Wires had been attached to all the shingles where he lived and high-voltage antennae were laced throughout the attic. Powerful signals were being sent from a distant state and picked up by the wires and antennae and sent into his body. When these signals were sent out, Henry was transformed into a black rubber ball helpless to protect himself. He was bounced up and down and all around unable to control himself and completely at the mercy of the foreign agents.

Henry suddenly stopped in telling his story to get my reaction. He looked at me intently and said "You don't believe me, do you?"

I answered, "You believe what you are saying and that's what's important. It isn't important what I believe."

He seemed relieved. "That's okay., I don't care what you believe as long as you accept the fact I believe what I've told you."

For many sessions thereafter, Henry's delusions continued, were elaborated on or changed, or were absent. It was helpful to Henry for him to be allowed to talk without interruption or comment. It was a pleasant surprise after about six months of weekly sessions that Henry seemed quite lucid and capable of carrying on a rational conversation. He said he did not believe what he had told me, at least at this time. For the first time, he began to speak of his home and his family and the guilt he felt because of his behavior toward his loved ones. The opportunity for pastoral counseling had finally arrived. Together, we began to help Henry distinguish the irrational guilt he felt because of behavior he could not control because of his mental illness and the rational guilt he felt for behavior that he knew was wrong at the time and he had deliberately acted out in, what was to him, an immoral manner. Counseling helped Henry overcome his irrational guilt; confessions helped Henry to overcome his rational guilt. I was happy when other staff members at the hospital indicated that Henry's condition was improving and was due, at least in part, to the results of our pastoral counseling sessions.

This relationship continued until Henry was released from the hospital. One day I was informed that Henry's condition was, at least temporarily, in remission. He was released from the hospital and sent to a halfway house where he remained for several months. He continued to improve, although it was necessary for him to continue regular medication.

Many years later, I saw Henry. He now had a job in a factory and was living with a cousin who also worked in the factory. He seemed quite content; there had been no serious recurrence of his condition. He recalled, with unusual clarity, the various delusions and stories that he had told me. Then, I learned an important lesson: He told me how important it was to him to have had me listen to him without making fun of him or challenging his delusions. Only after he felt safe with me and able to talk about his delusions that it became possible to talk more rationally and lucidly about other matters, particularly his guilt feelings. He indicated that he firmly believed the alleviation of his guilt feelings was an important factor contributing to his presently arrested mental illness. Together, we prayed it might remain permanently in remission.

Unfortunately, the pastoral counselor must be a realist and accept the fact that many cases involving thinking disorders do not go into remission or seem to change. However, I learned a lesson from dealing with Henry. Many times when he talked delusionally, it seemed he was completely out of touch with reality. This was not necessarily so. He told me he "remembered everything that was said every time we met and thought about our talks many times between sessions." The counselor, then, can never know what effect his counseling and empathic understanding can mean, even in seemingly hopeless cases. There may be a time or times when the patient understands and benefits from the relationship, even though there seems to be little change in his or her thinking. In addition, the counselor may be unaware of the client's ability to understand at the time. A counselor may well remember the adage "He also serves who only stands and waits."

Carol

As a high school English teacher in a small town, I knew the Jordan family very well. Mrs. Jordan was a hardworking seamstress, a widow with seven children. When I first met the family, five of the children were grown and were on their own. Only two were still in school; Horace, a senior in my class, and Carol, the youngest child, in the tenth grade. I came to know them because of my relationship with Horace. He seemed to like me and was willing to talk. He was somewhat shy and certainly lacking in self-esteem and self-confidence when I met him. He wanted to go to college, but he was convinced he did not have the mental ability to succeed. With Horace's permission, I asked the school psychologist about him and found that he had better than average intelligence and could make it in college if he developed some self-confidence. Through his senior year we worked on his problem. He was convinced that he could make it. He enrolled in college, and, on his visits home, he enjoyed my having dinner with him and his mother and his sister, Carol, while he related with pride his success in college. He was preparing to be a vocational counselor.

Carol enrolled in my English class in her senior year. She had poor grades, and it was doubtful if she would ever graduate. Carol was a shy, quiet, and withdrawn young woman. She had no friends and sat, most of the time, silently by herself. At no time did she volunteer or participate willingly in class activities or discussions. She seemed to be living in her own dream world, remote and apart from her peers and other associates.

Mrs. Jordan came to me one day and asked me to try and help Carol; she had done all she could but was unable to reach or understand Carol's inner and personal world. I said I would try, but I first would like permission to have a report on Carol from the school psychologist. Both Carol and her mother agreed. I was unhappy when the report came that Carol was suffering from a thinking disorder sometimes called *adolescent schizophrenia*. The school psychologist felt that she should be hospitalized, at least for awhile. She suggested that, through hospitalization and treatment, the prognosis would be good for eventual recovery.

With some personal misgivings, I approached Mrs. Jordan about possible placement of Carol in the inpatient treatment center at the local mental health clinic. Mrs. Jordan was stunned, and when Horace heard about it, his angry comment was, "I thought you liked us and wanted to help us. Instead, you want them to put my little sister away." It was clear the value systems of both Horace and his mother needed to be examined and changed.

Only when Carol said, "If you think I should go, I think you know best . . . I'll go." Horace and his mother consented to the hospitalization.

During the months that followed during Carol's hospitalization, Mrs. Jordan, Horace, and I discussed their respective value systems. They recognized, too, sometimes relatives and friends love someone "well but not wisely," as it would seem to have been in the case of Carol. Often, mistakenly, families and relatives protect a loved one against treatment, particularly in the case of emotional and mental illness, as well as with alcoholism and drug dependency. It was in the best interest of Carol to be hospitalized, even though there was a natural reluctance on the part of Horace and his mother to place her in a mental hospital. Faith and hope were seen to be virtually lacking in both their value systems. Further, these values systems were seen to be inadequate because they were based upon a weak and

faulty religious philosophy and theology. Each needed to in-
corporate in his or her value system the virtues of faith and
hope and the belief that a loving God would not allow such an
illness without cause and which could not lead ultimately to
good for Carol.

I visited Carol in the hospital several times. She responded
readily to medical and psychological treatment. A few months
after admission, she was helping the nurses and aides with the
older patients who were handicapped or in wheelchairs. She
was noticeably less withdrawn and enjoyed talking and helping
the older patients. In less than a year, Carol was released from
the hospital. She returned to her studies and enthusiastically
looked forward to becoming a mental health technician and
nurse's aide.

Coletta

Brain damage, whether caused through injury, disease, alcoholism, drugs, or other reasons, can be traumatic for an individual and his or her loved ones. Often, value systems and
theologies are shown to be weak and ineffectual after such
injuries. This was true for Coletta and her family after she
incurred serious brain damage after a car accident.

At twenty-eight Coletta seemed to have a promising career as
a ballet dancer with a nationally known troupe. Her father was
an owner of a small restaurant. Both he and Coletta's mother
worked long hours seven days a week to earn the money for her
dancing lessons.

Tragedy struck when Coletta was returning from a performance in a nearby town. She was not driving the car but sitting
in the seat next to the driver. Suddenly, another car approached
from the opposite direction, veered across the median dividing
line, and collided head-on with the car in which Coletta was
riding. The driver was killed and Coletta thrown from the car
onto the pavement. Coletta was taken to the hospital bleeding
and unconscious. It was doubtful for several days whether she
would survive at all. She lived, but it was clear she would never
dance again. Injury to the left side of her brain had left her

almost totally paralyzed on her right side and in her right arm and leg. When she recovered sufficiently to learn of the extent of her injuries, she found it almost impossible to reconcile herself to her loss. It was feared that she might commit suicide. She was heard to say over and over again, "Why didn't I die rather than live a hopeless cripple? I don't want to live. There is nothing left to live for. I want to die. Please let me die."

I was the sister assigned to Coletta as her speical nurse. Long months of physical rehabilitation and psychological and spiritual adjustment lay ahead. She wished to see no one except her parents. I accepted the role not only to help her in her physical rehabilitation but, insofar as possible, to serve as her spiritual counselor.

For some time, I did nothing but listen to Coletta as she ventilated her feelings of despondency and hurt. I felt that simply being there, saying nothing, and letting her express herself was the best thing for me to do. No words of mine could restore her to her former self; expressions of sympathy seemed out-of-place and inadequate. Thus, for several weeks I helped her into her wheelchair, rolled her to the physical reconditioning room, and helped her with the exercises prescribed for her. Naturally, I did not remain completely silent but talked with her when she wished to come out of her self-pitying loneliness to communicate with another human being.

It was about one month after I began caring for Coletta that she seemed to change somewhat. Calmly, one day, she asked me for my opinion: "Why did this have to happen to me? Why?"

Based upon my own theology and value system, I answered honestly, "I don't know. It is a mystery to me. However, I am convinced that a loving God would not let something like this happen for no good reason. It's just that at the time something like this happens we don't know, ultimately, why, but I am convinced — and I hope you are — that if one can accept it, God can turn it into good."

"That's easier said than done; I'm not sure that I can accept it," Coletta replied.

We said little more on the subject for sometime, but it was clear that Coletta was doing a great deal of thinking. Hopefully, she was reforming her theological value system, which up to now was clearly inadequate for such a crisis.

As the days went on, Coletta began to talk less and less about herself. One day, to my surprise, she turned to me as I was wheeling her out of the exercise room and said, "You know, I really feel sorry for those little paraplegics who are brought to the exercise room each day. They are so young — and so helpless. At least I know how it felt to walk and use my arms. Some of them have never walked and have never had the use of their hands. . . . Yes, I feel very sorry for them. It seems strange, though, they seem to be happy, and I've never heard one of them complain. They really are something." Again, I said very little but let Coletta know that I too understood and loved these children.

As the days passed, Coletta seemed more and more to accept her condition. She talked of the children more and more. She asked for books discussing paraplegia. Finally, one day, with marked enthusiasm, she blurted out to me, "Sister, I'm going to become a rehabilitation specialist for paraplegic children. I can't think of anything in the world I'd rather do. I know I can become one, even though I have to go to school in a wheelchair. At least my brain is not damaged in a way that I cannot learn. I'm thankful to God for that."

During the next three years, Coletta lived at home, confined most of the day to her wheelchair. Once a week she came back to the hospital for treatment and to report her progress in training to be a rehabilitation specialist. From her fellow students came glowing reports of the effect her pleasant and cheerful ways had on the whole group and the compassion and understanding she showed to the children she served during her internship.

It was a proud day for her parents, Coletta, and me when she graduated. Soon thereafter, she became a therapist, a happy and useful woman, in a rehabilitation center for children. In catechism I learned, "God works in mysterious ways; his marvels to perform." It seemed this was true in the case of Coletta.

Lawrence

I had been the pastor of a church in a small suburb of Chicago for nearly twenty years. I had seen babies I had baptized grow to adulthood. I had buried the church people's relatives and married their children. The pastoral care necessary was varied and never the same for any two people. I had not been trained professionally as a counselor, but I found I spent a great deal of time teaching and instructing as well as counseling.

One evening as I sat in my study, I heard a knock on the door. I went to the door and there stood a seedy-looking, poorly dressed man. His hands shook as he stood there, and when he spoke, he stuttered and stammered slightly. After a few moments, he said, "I'm sure you don't remember me, do you?" I confessed I did not. "Well, I'm Lawrence Spivey; I guess I don't look like I did when you last saw me ten years ago."

To say the least, I was shocked. The Lawrence Spivey I had known ten years before when he left for Chicago was a handsome young man of thirty-nine who had become a successful lawyer and was joining a large law office in the city. I said to myself, "How can this disheveled man, who looks years older than his almost fifty years of age, be Lawrence Spivey?" He interrupted my musing and asked if he could come in. I said he might and together we went to my study.

Lawrence then told me his story. After he left our community, he joined the law firm in the city. For a while everything went well; he was successful and entertained and wined and dined in the finest circles. Almost unnoticed, at first, the luncheon cocktails began to increase, and the evening cocktail hour extended so that in time dinner did not follow. Within two years, Lawrence was carrying a bottle to the office to be kept in his desk where he could take a drink during office hours. It was not long until he had to have a drink or two or three when he arose in the morning before going to the office. His colleagues noticed that he was drinking more and more, but rather than suggesting that he might have an alcohol problem, they protected him, even against himself, by finding excuses for his drinking.

Lawrence had a modest annuity he received from his father's estate each year. He reasoned that he could quit work and live — and drink — as he saw fit. Thus, after three years he "retired." For the next six years, Lawrence confided, he was rarely sober, and the annuity he received went largely for booze. In time he landed on skid row, did nothing but drink, and slept at night on a park bench.

Then one year, before he came to see me, he found himself lying in a hospital. He had been picked up by the police while he was in a blackout, a condition in which he could remember nothing. The attendants at the hospital told him that he had had a severe attack of delirium tremens. They suggested that not only should he do something about his alcohol addiction, but he also should have both a physical and mental examination for possible damage. For the first time, Lawrence accepted the fact that he was addicted to alcohol; he resolved to seek help through Alcoholics Anonymous. From them, he learned that alcoholism is an addiction for which a person is not responsible and for which an individual need feel no shame. They did teach him, however, that there is no known cure for alcoholism and that he must learn to control his addiction by abstinence for the rest of his life. Since that day, Lawrence related, he had been a faithful participant in the AA program in his neighborhood.

Alcoholics Anonymous had become a lifesaver for Lawrence; through it, he learned to control his addiction and abstain from alcohol. One thing, however, that AA could not do was repair the damage that alcohol had done to Lawrence physically and mentally. He now had evident liver damage, and, even more important to him, the neurologists had indicated mild to moderate brain damage. This, he explained, was the reason he could not control his hands from shaking and the reason for his slurred speech.

I then asked him how I could help him at this time. He answered, "I have made such a mess of my life, sometimes I have felt like giving up, but my faith won't let me, so I have come to you for help. I know that I am unable to return to law practice — that's the price I must pay — I can't handle, intellectually, such matters anymore. I go blank at times and simply cannot reason as well as I once was able to do. I am a realist, however; my brain is damaged so that I cannot function as I did when you knew me ten years ago. However, it could be worse."

Pastoral counseling of Lawrence was done in three stages. The first stage involved the alleviation of guilt that Lawrence felt. Through his AA participation, he felt no irrational guilt for his alcohol addiction; he felt guilty for many things he had done sober or partially sober that violated his moral code. This guilt was handled in the usual manner (rational versus irrational guilt).

The second stage of the counseling involved looking back into the past to see what could be salvaged in terms of values, goals, interests, and aspirations. Although it was clear that he could never return to law practice, it developed that Lawrence's interest in law was based primarily on his concern for other people and justice and the rights of all human beings. This, we found, could continue to be an important part of his value system and could lead to other alternatives through which Lawrence could serve human beings and their needs.

Lawrence initiated and determined the third stage of the counseling relationship. It had occurred to him that even though his ability to speak was no longer perfect, he could communicate from a platform to an audience. He could think of no better way to spend his life than volunteering to talk to high school assemblies church groups, and teenage clubs and groups about the effects of the use of drugs and alcohol on the human being. He recognized that his shaky hands and slurred speech might be, at times, a source of ridicule. He was willing to take that chance, for he reasoned that his own physical and mental condition as a result of alcohol addiction might tell a more poignant story than anything he might say.

This was a practical alternative life-style from practicing law and involved realistic and attainable goals for Lawrence. Fortunately, he was financially able because of his annuity, if he lived modestly, to devote his entire time to volunteer work with youth groups. Together, we planned a stategy for introducing

Lawrence to many and varied groups of young people.

I learned later that rarely was there anything but an enthusiastic reception given Lawrence. His influence on potential young addicts cannot be measured, but it was clear, life had taken on a new and richly rewarding meaning for Lawrence as he gained back his own self-esteem and contributed to the value systems of the young. He told me he took as a daily motto and reminder a passage from the poem *If* by Rudyard Kipling: "If you can watch the things you gave your life to broken, and stoop to build them up with worn-out tools. . . . Yours is the earth and everything that's in it, and what is more you'll be a man, my son."

Strictly speaking, the cases of Coletta and Lawrence do not involve cases of atypical thinking but cases of impaired thinking. However, they are presented so that the pastoral counselor can understand his or her valuable role, particularly in aiding individuals with brain damage, specifically in developing adequate value systems and determining realistic goals after such impairment.

Dr. Albert Scott

One of the most difficult and painful experiences for anyone is to watch a brilliant and talented man or woman deteriorate mentally as they grow old. The case of Dr. Scott is such a case.

For thirty-five years, Dr. Scott had a busy and thriving practice as a general practitioner and surgeon. He was devoted to his patients and they were to him.

At seventy-five, Dr. Scott lived with his wife Margaret, a former nurse, in their large home. All their children were grown and had moved away with their families to other cities.

Even at his advanced age, Dr. Scott continued his daily practice of medicine. I was not aware that anything was wrong until Margaret came to see me.

She sat silently in my office for a few minutes and then began to cry softly. When her tears had subsided, I listened as Margaret talked about her husband. She said that he had always been a thoughtful husband and a good father to their five children. Lately, however, he seemed to have changed. Not only did he forget where things were, but he would stop in the middle of a sentence as if he had lost his train of thought. More than that, he had become suspicious of everyone with whom Margaret talked. Several times she caught him hiding behind the door when she had a visitor. Afterwards, he would question her: "What did Helen say about me? Was Jack talking about me? Did Carl say something against me?" Such questions were asked of everyone who came to the house.

Margaret had tried to cover up the doctor's condition, but a change in his personality and behavior was becoming more evident in his office. He had become forgetful and grouchy and often seemed unaware of what was going on. Margaret feared not only for him but for the potential danger to his patients. She did not know what to do and therefore had come to me for advice and counsel.

I suggested that she should convince Albert to go to a specialist to see if there was something wrong. Margaret informed me that he absolutely refused to see any other doctor or specialist. I then asked her if I might consult a neurologist and discuss the situation in confidence. She agreed, and we set a date for our next meeting.

I went to see the neurologist, Dr. Pike, and was informed that in all probability Dr. Scott's condition was serious. Naturally, Dr. Pike could not be sure without an examination. However, he suggested the symptoms sounded like possibly the beginning of *senile dementia,* a condition for which there is no known cure and which, in many cases, becomes progressively worse with age. He suggested that Dr. Scott should retire and that those around him should expect increasing self-centeredness, difficulty in assimilating new experiences, and frequent outbreaks of childish emotionality, jealousy, and suspicion.

It was my painful duty to tell Margaret the facts. Unexpectedly, Margaret refused to accept reality and became angry with me when I suggested that he retire. "How could I suggest such a thing! Think of his reputation! I'm sure he will get better." She thanked me and stormed out of my office. I did not see her again for two months.

Margaret finally came to my office obviously tired, upset, and in pain. "I can't keep it up any longer," she sighed. "I'm becoming a nervous wreck myself. Albert now gets up in the middle of the night — often several times — and wanders aimlessly about the house. I doubt that he knows what he is doing. Also, lately he has begun to lose control of his bladder and his bowels. Even though I'm a trained nurse, it is a terrible strain." She paused for a moment. Then she asked me, "I don't want to offend Albert and suggest that he retire. I'm a coward. Would you come to dinner some night and help me with this difficult thing?" I said yes, and arrangements were made. Such a meeting with Albert and Margaret was not unusual, since I had dined many times in their home.

It was much easier to convince Albert that he should retire than was expected. At the table we discussed the many successful years of practice Albert had enjoyed and the reputation he had with everyone in the community. Finally, I said, "Albert, you've worked so hard for so many years, don't you think Margaret and you have a right to enjoy a few years by yourself? I'm sure Margaret would agree." I turned to Margaret. She nodded assent.

Albert looked at both of us for several seconds and then slowly answered, "You know what, I've been wanting to retire for a long time. I'm just plain tired and I can't remember things like I used to. I know what's really wrong with me — you see, I am a doctor and I know what can happen in advancing old age. To tell the truth, I only stayed on because I thought Margaret, my wonderful wife, wanted me to continue. I've always wanted her to be proud of me. She means so much in my life." He paused and then turned to Margaret — by the slightest motion of her head, she again indicated her approval.

As it happened, Albert was not the one who needed counseling but the one who sought help for him, his wife, Margaret. I asked her to see me regularly each week, and she agreed. At first, we looked back together and looked at the "tracks" and accomplishments this man and woman had made. They had raised a fine family; together they had contributed to the lives of countless individuals; they now enjoyed an enviable reputation in the community and with all the townspeople. No sickness or impairment could take away or diminsh these accomplishments and contributions to those around them.

Then, we looked forward; this was the hardest thing for Margaret to do. That is, to face the reality of old age and the accompanying physical and sometimes mental and emotional problems that are, often, a part of the aging process. Yes, she must alter her value system and strengthen her religious convictions so that she could face old age and the inevitability of death for both herself and her husband. More importantly, she needed to live existentially, in the present. Cherishing the accomplishments and joys of the past and dispassionately accepting the facts of old age and ultimately death was not enough. She needed to live fully each moment of the present without reference either to the past or the future.

It was difficult for Margaret to adjust to a new value system, but in time she did so. Retirement for Albert seemed to somewhat arrest his condition. Many evenings I would see Albert and Margaret holding hands as they sat in their garden, just being together. Albert lived five years after he retired. Margaret was prepared when the end came.

Part III
Atypical Feelings and
Emotional Behavior

CHAPTER 5

SEVERE ATYPICAL FEELINGS
AND EMOTIONAL BEHAVIOR

INTRODUCTION

BECAUSE mankind evidences an increasingly
large number of atypical feelings and emotional behavior, these
are considered under three headings in the chapters that follow:
(1) severe, often called *psychotic* or *affective emotional disorders;* (2) the large and varied group of atypical feelings, gen-
erally known as *neuroses;* and (3) the special cases of emotional
feelings known as *depression,* considered with the pastoral
counselor's role where there is a possibility of suicide.

At the outset, the pastoral counselor should understand that
nearly all the cases discussed require other professional treatment and therapy from clinical psychologists, psychiatrists,
and/or physicians. The main purpose, therefore, of these chapters is to enable the counselor *to recognize* the disorders, make
proper referrals, and be available for consultation and for counseling. It is possible, subsequent to the referral, that the pastoral counselor may work along with clinical or medical
professionals while they are in therapy or following treatment.
In no area does the pastoral counselor make a bigger mistake
than attempting, without further training, to handle the problems of these individuals, for the roots of the trouble are usually deep-seated physical or psychological disorders. Only in
those cases where it is evident that guilt and/or values is the
basic problem should the counselor attempt to treat a client
alone. In some cases, however, when a client refuses to go to
another professional, it may be the task of the pastor to work
with the individual for some time until he or she is willing to
seek treatment. Many times a person comes to a counselor,
particularly if he is a priest or minister, before anyone else. The

49

skill needed, then, is in supporting the individual and using every reasonable means to encourage and direct the person to the proper clinical or medical professional.

Severe Atypical Feelings

Some individuals suffer from severe atypical feelings called *psychotic affective responses*. Two are of primary importance: *manic* and *depressive reactions*. Both are characterized by the following: (1) inappropriate elation or sadness in a given situation, and (2) usually, a lack of anxiety connected with such response or no recognition by the person that the response is inappropriate. Crying profusely at a happy wedding celebration and laughing inordinately at a funeral are such responses. There are many different emotional reactions that are inappropriate in any given situation. The causes are unknown. However, the conditions are treatable, even though the condition may never be completely cured.

When someone comes to a pastoral counselor and evidences such atypical feelings and emotions, the individual should be referred to an appropriate medical professional. In turn, he or she will decide if hospitalization is necessary. In many cases, whether the individual is hospitalized or not, the physician prescribes drugs for the person: tranquilizers for manic disorders and stimulants for depressive conditions. It is important, however, that the individual be encouraged to remain in constant contact with the doctor, not only to regulate medical dosages, but because of the possibility of a mood swing, which often occurs. It is common for an individual who has been showing manic emotions to suddenly swing to a depressed reaction. It is crucial that the physician be able to adjust the medication for the patient if such mood changes occur.

After the patient has proper medication and possibly psychotherapy with a trained clinician, a pastoral counselor may then be able to contribute to the well-being of the person, as the following cases demonstrate. Briefly, then, it is the pastoral counselor's role to (1) recognize the symptoms of these severe emotional disorders, (2) refer the patient to the proper medical and clinical professionals, and (3) be available as a consultant and possible counselor after the emotional condition is under control.

In terms of the procedures recommended earlier, the preliminary assessment then becomes critically important in these cases to determine the competency of the pastoral counselor.

Kenneth

Case Presentation

I was somewhat apprehensive on my first visit to a state mental hospital. As a seminarian, I had been assigned as my field work to go once a week and spend two hours at the institution, one with the staff for training and one hour visiting patients. My first experience with an individual who was hospitalized because of manic behavior was with Kenneth. I was assured by the staff that he was under sedation and other medications and would not be dangerous. It was left to me to determine my own approach to him.

Procedures

When I met Kenneth, I found him to be a tall, somewhat gaunt man about thirty or thirty-five years old. When I shook hands with him, he looked puzzled, as if to find out why I was here. I felt telling him the truth was my best approach. I explained that I was studying for the ministry and that I wanted to learn how best to serve all people that I might meet, including those in hospitals.

Kenneth seemed satisfied with my explanation for my presence. Soon, he began to talk rapidly but coherently about himself. I decided to use what my professors had called reality counseling; that is, to let Kenneth talk about his world as he saw it without interruption.

Counseling and Discussion

Kenneth told me that he and his sister had lived with his

divorced mother during the early years of their lives. He did not remember his father. He was his mother's favorite and was allowed to do as he pleased. She rarely, if ever, disciplined him, even though he remembered hearing a doctor once say that he was "overactive" and that his mother should do something about it. "Mother wouldn't hear of it, even though I was always restless and running around a lot every day. I was real tired at night." My being restless got worse as I began to grow to a man — you know what I mean. Sometimes I felt I was on fire and had to run to put the fire out. Other times I felt I was going to explode if I couldn't let out the steam. I practically died each night, I was so tired from tearing around. Also, it was almost impossible for me to sit still in a school classroom. That's one of the reasons I quit when I was in the tenth grade. My mother didn't seem to mind. She let me go to work with a construction crew, but I didn't keep the job long because the boss said I made everyone nervous by my talking and acting so much. I went from one job to another. When I was eighteen, my mother died, my sister went to live with an aunt, and I drifted to the city. I never could keep a job and the steam inside of me kept building up and building up. No matter what I did, I couldn't get rid of it.

"Then, one day I was shooting pool with some guys I knew, and one of them cheated me. Something broke loose inside of me. The next thing I know'd, the police had me handcuffed and one of my buddies is on the way to the hospital in an ambulance because I hit him hard with a chair. Thank God, he didn't die, but he almost did." Kenneth paused for a brief moment and then continued. "What happened then for some time I don't really know. It's all hazy. All I know is that I was told I was moved from jail and placed here. I had to be strapped down for sometime, and I had some treatment. I think it's called 'shock.' They tell me I have been here for two months; however, I don't remember much until about a couple of weeks ago. The doctor says the pills they are giving me to quiet my nerves are doing great things for me, and I guess he's right, because I don't feel so uptight as I used to. He even said if I keep getting better, I don't have to stay here too long . . . that is, if I keep taking my pills and coming to see him sometimes."

For several sessions, Kenneth continued to ventilate his feelings and talk about his world. After four visits, we began to talk about his future. Without his recognizing it as such, we began to talk about his value system. He indicated he did not mind work and he would like to live at peace with himself and with people around him. He had a primitive faith: He had no doubt that God existed and that he rewarded the good and punished the bad. He wanted to be good so that people would like him and God would love him, too. He expressed one concern that we had to deal with in our counseling sessions.

Kenneth was not sure God would forgive him for almost killing a man and hurting others as he had in the poolroom. I was able to explain to him that God does not hold us responsible for actions that were not done deliberately. As I told him, I was taught in Sunday School that for an action to be wrong in the eyes of God, it had to be something serious that is known to be wrong and, more importantly, it has to be done deliberately. I asked him if he really felt he had deliberately hurt anyone. He shook his head no. Nevertheless, he said, "I still feel bad about what I have did." It was decided that we would kneel down together and ask "real hard" for God to forgive him for anything that he had done wrong. This simple act seemed to relieve and satisfy Kenneth.

Evaluation and Results

Several months later, Kenneth was discharged from the hospital. Our relationship had changed. It was no longer a relationship of counselor and client but of two friends. It was decided that Kenneth should go to work on a farm nearby and live with the family there. Such work would channel Kenneth's seemingly inexhaustible energy in a positive and constructive direction. To the best of my knowledge, Kenneth found himself, peace, and what he wanted on the farm. "Come unto me all ye that labor and are heavy laden and I will give you rest." (Matt. 11:28)

Nellie

Case Presentation

I was a social caseworker assigned to visit the squalid homes in a small mining town. The work was hard but gratifying, since so much could be done for these poor people.

On one of my visits I met Nellie. She was a woman probably in her forties but who looked much older. She and her unmarried older sister and brother all lived together in a three-room house; one room was the kitchen, dining, and living room. There were two bedrooms. There was no inside water or plumbing. The only financial support they had was from the meagre funds Ted, Nellie's brother, brought home from his work in the coal mines. It was to their credit, however, that they remained as clean as possible and never complained.

I became disturbed on my first visit with Nellie. She sat in the corner, said nothing, and never looked up at me but stared constantly at the floor. I mentioned this to her sister, Cora, as I began to leave. I asked if I had done something. "No," said Cora, "She sits like that day in and day out. Sometimes she begins to cry, and we don't know why. All she says is 'I'm going to die' or some silly nonsense 'that 'I'm dead and the worms are already eating my flesh.' " I suggested that Nellie should be examined by a doctor. Cora would have none of it. "We take care of our own," she said. "We always have and always will." At this point, I could do nothing more.

On my next visit, I was surprised to see that Nellie was not there. When I asked about her, Cora explained that Nellie had tried to kill herself and the doctor had recommended she be placed in a hospital for treatment. It was after she entered the hospital that a counseling relationship was established between the two of us.

Procedures

I did not see Nellie for three weeks after she was admitted to the hospital. I was informed that she had responded almost miraculously to a series of electroshock treatments and a combination of antidepressant and antianxiety drugs.

I was surprised when I entered the room. Nellie looked up immediately and said, "Hello, I'm glad you came to see me." Since it seemed she wanted to talk, I decided my best approach would be to listen and comment only when she wished me to do so.

Counseling and Discussion

At first, our conversations centered around Nellie's life with Ted and Cora. It took some time for us to talk about Nellie herself. The first three conversations seemed to be going nowhere, but I had been taught to be patient. I resolved, however that on the next session we would talk about Nellie, her ideals, values, and ambitions.

I began the session by saying, "Now, Nellie you have told me a great deal about your family, but I want to hear something about you, and what you like and want to do in life."

Nellie sat for a few moments, and then, almost in pain she answered me, "To tell the truth, I don't think I'm much of anything . . . that's one of my biggest troubles. I don't feel anyone needs me and I'm just in the way. Cora looks after the house, does the cooking and the laundry for both Ted and me. Ted's a good man and a hardworking one. He makes a living for all of us in those dirty old coal mines. I think he's developing what is known as 'black lung,' but he won't quit, for he says he doesn't know how to do anything but work in the mines. Me, I don't do anything. I guess I don't have much to offer anyone. That's one reason I always have felt down in the dumps. I feel useless." She paused. It was clear she had a poor self-concept and felt there was no reasons for her existence. In addition, she felt she was a nuisance and a burden to her brother and sister. It became our task together to build her self-esteem and feeling of self- and personal worth.

We began by reading scripture together. It convinced Nellie

that God made everyone uniquely and had a reason for creation of every living being. There was, therefore, a plan and reason for Nellie's being. Thus, the first step in pastoral counseling had been achieved.

Once Nellie was convinced that she was someone created by God to be respected by herself and by others, we began to look into her interests, potential talents, and abilities. Nellie had not had much formal education, but she loved beautiful things and was good with her hands. It was decided that she might try knitting and crocheting, so we got the necessary yarn and other supplies. It occurred to her that she would like to become skilled so that she could make a sweater for Ted and a shawl for Cora and other necessities for their home. After deciding on this purpose, Nellie seemed to become a different person. With enthusiasm, she spent several hours each day learning to perfect her newfound interest.

Evaluation and Results

As Nellie improved, we looked forward to the day when she could return to her home. She had knitted a gift for both Ted and Cora. She wanted to surprise them, and she did. They were delighted when she gave each of them the gift she had made. She, too, felt important. At this point, she resolved to do all the sewing for the family.

In the years that followed, Nellie still needed medication, but she had a purpose for living. She became a contented woman. She was always shy and avoided crowds, but she needed no one but her family. She became a very religious woman, reading her Bible each day. The balance of the time she sewed and took care of Ted and Cora's clothing and other needs. She took as her Biblical motto, "God is our refuge and strength, a very present help in trouble. Therefore will not we fear." (Ps. 46:1, 2)

Leo

As a new chaplain at the state mental hospital, I was interested to know that the majority of the patients, especially those who remained at least for a long time or for life, were suffering primarily from schizophrenic thinking disorders. I learned that only 2 percent of first admissions were manic or depressive or both in their behavior. Of these, due to increasingly important chemotherapy, only a small percentage had to remain in the institution for any length of time or for life. Leo, however, was to become one of the permanent residents. It was impossible to regulate medications. One day, he would be elated and manic, needing tranquilizers; the following day, depressed and needing stimulants. There was no set pattern for his mood swings and no way to predict what his mood would be at any given time.

I wondered how I could serve as a pastoral counselor for Leo. I decided I should listen to him both when he was "high" and when he was "low." By doing so, I was able to find ways to minister to him.

One day, when I came to Leo's room, he was very depressed, hardly wishing to talk, although I had known him for several weeks. Finally, with deep sighs, he talked of dying, his puny physical build, his lack of education, and his lack of ambition. It was at this time and in subsequent depressive periods that I used a type of reinforcement counseling. I repeatedly assured him that he was worth something, that life could have meaning for him, regardless of his physical, emotional, or other handicaps. It seemed to register with him when I would say, "Do you think I would waste my time spending this time with you if I didn't think you were worth something and were important?" I continued, "I wish you thought as much of yourself as I do and the rest of the staff here. We are trying to help you because we like you and believe in you. You need to do the same thing."

It was different when Leo was excited and agitated. It was soon clear we needed to find an outlet for his energy in a constructive rather than self-destructive way. To find this took some time. Together, we explored his past interests and his potential abilities. It was found that he liked to work with his hands and had a flare for painting. It was decided it would be therapeutic for Leo to paint — to paint anything he wished, no matter how grotesque or unreal the painting might be.

His early attempts were bizarre. His clinician said, however, it helped him understand the pyschological dynamics in Leo's case. As he continued to paint, he began to read and study more about art. He became quite good, if only in an amateur way. It was a proud day when he presented me with a painting he had done for me. When he saw the genuine pleasure it gave me, he relaxed as I had never seen him do. He was finding his way to self-expression; more than that, to a feeling of belonging and being useful. It was significant that the painting depicted a deity holding a large number of men and women from different races in his hand as if to support and sustain them. This was expressed during his period of elation; however, the theme was clearly based upon our counseling sessions when he had been depressed.

To my knowledge, Leo was never able to leave the hospital. However, with his new skill and self-confidence, his mood swings became progressively less violent. His medications decreased, and he became a favorite among the staff in the institution, not only for his paintings but also for his cooperative attitude.

Often, a pastoral counselor may feel he or she is not doing much for such a patient. This is not true, however, from the point of view of the client, who is the final judge of the effectiveness of the counseling relationship.

CHAPTER 6

NEUROTIC FEELINGS AND BEHAVIOR

BY far the largest number and most varied kinds of atypical feelings and behavior are known as *neuroses.*

In a very real sense, every human being is neurotic to a lesser or greater degree. Basically, neurotic feelings and behavior are attempts to compensate or displace anxiety created by the stresses and strains in everyday life that cannot be dissipated completely or at all through adaptive or semiadaptive means and mechanisms.

Frustrations, conflicts, and pressures create the anxiety. To the degree this psychological "stream" remains in the human organism, he or she remains to some degree anxious and tense. In most cases, however, this anxiety and tension does not interfere in a serious way with a person's life. When it interferes in a significant manner or leads to atypical feelings and behavior for a given society, it is technically called *neurosis.*

There are three main characteristics of neurosis that can easily be recognized by the pastoral counselor: (1) Anxiety and tension is usually present. (2) Symptomatically, there is some form of irrational feeling or behavior. (3) The individual recognizes that his behavior is irrational but does not know what is the basic problem underlying the neurotic behavior or how to overcome it. Only in rare cases for example, when the basic problem involves guilt, is the pastoral counselor able to handle the underlying problem and the anxiety and tension evoking the neurotic behavior. Treatment for these is the special and specific professional role of the clinical psychologist or other therapist.

Fortunately, the prognosis for treatment of neurotic behavior is good. Between 40 and 60 percent of patients recover spontaneously or with a minimum of psychotherapy. With the help of the trained clinician, many more can be treated successfully. In most cases, therefore, the first duty of the pastoral counselor is to recognize neurotic behavior and to refer the individual to a clinician. Specifically, when a tense and anxious person, one who recognizes that his or her feelings and behavior are irrational but does not know the cause or how to overcome them, comes to the pastoral counselor, he or she should be referred for therapy.

The symptomatic behavior is easy to recognize. However, it takes many forms. For example, it may lead to phobias, such as fear of heights, open places, pain, thunder, storms, lightning, closed places, blood, germs, being alone, darkness, crowds, disease, fire, animals, or a particular animal, etc. On the other hand, the person may feel chronic mental and physical fatigue or present with symptoms of a physical illness without any underlying organic pathology. In still other cases, it may lead to what is known as *amnesia,* which involves either partial or total inability to recall past experiences. It may also lead instead to sleepwalking or in many cases to an uneasiness caused by what is known as *free-floating anxiety.*

The two most common neuroses account for over 50 to 60 percent of all neurotic conditions. These are (1) *obsessive-compulsive behavior,* which is important to those in religion, for it includes scrupulosity as a common form of this behavior; and (2) *depressive neurotic reactions,* which may involve potential suicide. Special attention, therefore, is given these two forms of neurotic behavior. Depression and suicide are so important they warrant a separate chapter.

Referral for psychotherapy where it is possible is the first obligation of the pastoral counselor. However, this is not the only role the counselor can play in the lives of these people in pain. In many cases, he or she will be asked to serve as a consultant and co-worker with the psychotherapist. This is ideal, wherever it is possible, for as the guilt surfaces in psychotherapy, the pastoral counselor is available to assist in alleviation of the guilt. Of equal importance, in most cases, the neurosis has been caused by faulty or arrested personality development. The psychotherapist can help the patient to realize his or her problem, but often it is the pastoral counselor who can help the client-patient to enriched self-esteem and self-acceptance based upon an adequate theology and value system. Often, he can guide the individual to a more realistic, mature, and adequate self-concept based upon the conviction of the worth, dignity, and value of each human being.

It is the pastoral counselor who assists the individual in reevaluating and assessing his values and goals and helps him develop realistic goals and energizing, creative, and sustaining values for the future.

Louise

Louise, a pretty but shy university student, often came to me, a vocational counselor, to talk. She seemed to need constant support and an opportunity to discuss her real and imaginary problems.

Louise was an only child. Her mother was a cold and domineering woman, while her father was a meek little man who adored Louise and let her have anything she wanted or do what she wished. In his eyes, she could do no wrong.

Louise was not doing as well in her classes as one might expect. She was intelligent, but her emotional and personal problems seemed to block an optimal performance. One of her friend's suggested a reason: "She's a worry-wart, always worrying about something."

It was true; Louise seemed to have inumerable complaints and problems. One day, she would discuss her inability to sleep; the next day her bad habit of nail-biting; on another day her health and her fear of contagious diseases and cancer. She was particularly concerned about her appearance: She was never satisfied, although she spent hours on her makeup and in dressing. What others thought about her seemed the most important thing in the world. She worried constantly about the impression she made on her classmates, her teachers, the young men who visited her sorority house, and people in general, including chance acquaintances.

All my counseling seemed to accomplish little. I was genuinely interested in Louise but did not know how to help her. What to do came in an unexpected way.

Louise came to me one day crying hysterically. She had cried many times in her visits, but this seemed different. After her tears subsided somewhat, she sobbed as she told me what had happened.

She had walked into the meeting of her sorority, and Thelma, a girl she wanted as her best friend, began to laugh. Louise was crushed that Thelma was laughing at her. She dashed from the room, went to her room and cried, and as she could not stop, she came to me.

My first question was, "How do you know Thelma was laughing at you?"

Louise replied, "I just know so. She was looking right at me when she laughed."

I waited awhile and then made a decision. I said to her, "Louise, you know I think a great deal of you and I want what is best for you." She nodded in agreement. "I think you should go see a professional clinician for you need help. I can't give you the kind of professional help that a friend of mine, Dr. Ellis, a clinical psychologist, can. I'll be glad, however, to work with him if you will go — How about it?"

Louise replied, "Do you think I'm crazy and ought to be put away?

I quickly assured Louise I did not think so, but there are often problems we do not know how to solve on our own. I reminded her that she had said she felt many of her feelings, such as her fear and shyness, were irrational, but she didn't know why she felt the way she did or how to get rid of these feelings. She agreed that many times she felt her feelings were "silly" and she didn't know why she felt the way she did. Reluctantly, but with confidence in my advice, she sought the help of Dr. Ellis. It was agreed by Louise that the doctor and I could share confidences and serve as professional co-workers in her case.

When she went first for psychotherapy, I did not attempt to contact her or Dr. Ellis. He told me he would let me know when I should reenter the case. Louise saw him twice a week. I saw her frequently, but it was agreed that we would not go over what was done in the therapy sessions until Dr. Ellis wished us to do so.

Two months went by. One evening she came to see me to tell me how irrational and silly it was for her to think Thelma was laughing at her. Dr. Ellis, using rational behavior therapy, helped Louise substitute rational thinking for the irrational thinking that had led to her irrational emotions and response regarding Thelma. Louise said she then discussed the matter with Thelma and found out that someone had just told a joke and Thelma had said, "Louise will love it, just then you came in, and it made it even funnier."

The time came when Dr. Ellis, Louise, and I met together. Dr. Ellis explained that in the therapy sessions, it had become increasingly clear that Louise had a deep-seated feeling of inadequacy and dependency on others and their opinions. Dr. Ellis explained that this might be expected in the case of an only child who was not emotionally near to her mother but close to a doting father. For whatever reason, Louise felt insecure and inadequate. He suggested that the three of us might work together to help Louise develop self-confidence and independence. He indicated the final outcome of any therapy and counseling would be up to Louise: He and I would do our part, but she must do her part also.

I had many sessions with Louise. As it happened, we had similar religious backgrounds. It was my role to help her examine her faith and to reinforce those aspects of her religious beliefs that would increase her feeling of personal worth in her own viewpoint and that of her peers. More than that, that with God's help, she could learn a certain necessary independence and feeling of personal adequacy.

In the days that followed, many of Louise's neurotic symptoms disappeared. I was happy that by her senior year she seemed to worry little about herself and spent a good deal of her time and energy helping young, frightened, and often shy freshman students. I was delighted when she told me one day that she had decided to become a student and vocational counselor after she finished graduate school.

Pierre

It was my first experience as a student chaplain at a boy's

camp. The peaceful campsite in the foothills of the Catskills was in sharp contrast to the busy streets of Manhattan where I was attending school. The camp provided accommodations for seventy boys at one time; seven boys and a youth counselor (a high school senior) lived in each screened-in tent-house. A natural lake served as a swimming pool, and there was plenty of room for various athletic and recreational activities. My job was to conduct religious services each morning, look after the spiritual welfare of the boys, and help them keep in touch with their family through letters.

Things seemed to be going well, until Keith, one of the youth counselors, came to see me on our third day at the camp. He talked to me about one of the boys in his charge, the boy's name was Pierre. Keith told me that Pierre was "awfully" afraid of the dark. Each night Pierre would wake up screaming and ask that the lamp be turned on. Keith did so until Pierre went back to sleep, but it was only a few hours until it was necessary to turn the lamp on again. Neither Keith nor the other boys were able to get a good night's sleep as a result. I asked Keith to send Pierre to me.

When Pierre came into my tent-house, I surmised that he was about eleven years old. He was a well-developed, handsome young Frenchman with coal black hair, wearing a sweater and a French beret. I talked to Pierre and he admitted he was frightened by darkness, it terrified him. He was having trouble at the boy's school where he lived, so much so that the authorities had put him in a special room where a small light was left burning all night. Pierre did not know why he was so terrified by darkness. I did not know either, but I hoped to find out.

It was clear that Pierre needed to be moved from Keith's tent-house for his sake and the sake of the rest of the boys. I thought it would be best to allow Pierre to sleep on the other cot in my tent where I could leave a small candle burning all night. It would not bother my sleep, and it would help Pierre. He moved to my quarters and, with a light on, slept peacefully for the next few nights.

On Saturday afternoons I returned to New York City for

services on Sunday mornings and returned to camp on Sunday afternoon. Pierre traveled to and from New York on the same train. I learned from him that he went each weekend to visit his stepmother, a socialite in Manhattan. He told me he was born in France. His father deserted his mother before he was born and when he was four years of age his mother died. He was to be sent to an orphanage, but his uncle would not permit it. The uncle persuaded his American wife that they should adopt Pierre. She did not want children, since they would interfere with her social life, but was finally persuaded that it was the only thing to do. Pierre lived with his uncle and his wife until he was nine. His uncle was killed while skiing in the Alps, and his stepmother returned with Pierre to New York City. Pierre was placed in a boy's boarding school and saw his mother only on weekends.

On the first Saturday when we returned together to New York, I met Pierre's stepmother for the first time. She thanked me for being a companion for him to New York but indicated that he really did interfere with her personal and social life when he did come to see her. With a martyr's attitude, she took Pierre in tow for the rest of the day and night. She promised to have him back at the station in time for the train back to the camp on the following day.

On Sunday, Pierre's stepmother seemed relieved to see me there. She quickly turned him over to me so that she would not be late for a party she was going to attend.

Pierre and I sat in silence for some time. After a while I noticed large tears, which he tried to hold back, trickle down his face. Finally, somewhat tactlessly, I asked him what was the matter. He held back the tears as best he could and replied, "No one wants me . . . just no one." I did not need to be a professional to feel and understand the ache and hurt this lonely boy felt. I wondered if his neurotic fear of darkness might be related to his feeling of being unwanted and unloved. I determined to discuss the matter with a professional I knew at my first opportunity.

We returned to camp, and for the balance of his stay, Pierre slept on the cot in my tent. I talked to Dr. Comstock, a clinical psychologist, about Pierre. It was not possible for him to make an assessment of Pierre's neurotic behavior without seeing him, but, he suggested that in the proper environment — where he was felt loved and wanted — the phobia and other neurotic manifestations might disappear.

I determined to see his stepmother alone. She made it clear she would like to get rid of him but did not know how. I suggested that there were many childless couples looking for just such a boy as Pierre who would welcome becoming his foster parents. She agreed to let me look into it.

In the meantime, my role as pastoral counselor with Pierre was clear. He needed to know and feel that he was loved and wanted. He was a religious boy, so I began by assuring him that I knew God loved him or he would not have made him. It was natural, I explained, for him to feel unwanted as he did, since he had lost his own mother and father and his uncle and was now the ward of his stepmother, who did not understand his problem. However, there were many who loved him now and others would in the future. We spent many happy hours talking about what he liked and what he wanted to do in the future. He had always, he said, wanted to be a doctor, probably because the nicest persons he had met were me and a doctor he knew. Even at this early age, it was possible for Pierre and I not only to talk of his ambitions and goals but also his religious convictions and value system. He approached these with a greater maturity than one would expect in an eleven-year-old, perhaps because of the suffering he had known.

At the end of the summer, I made several contacts. A childless couple who had come from France met Pierre and loved him instantly. He was taken to their home, and in a short time he begged to be permitted to live with them. With his stepmother, we made the legal arrangements necessary. It was a rich experience for me and important for Pierre.

In the year that followed, I was curious about one thing. I asked the man and woman who had adopted him if he slept with a light on each night. Both looked at the other with a puzzled expression. They did not know he ever was afraid of the dark; he certainly had not been since he had come to live with them.

I was reminded as I thought of Pierre of the words of the Psalmist, "The Lord is my shepherd, I shall not want, He maketh me to lie down in green pastures . . . He restoreth my soul." (Ps. 23)

Mary Ann

Dr. Strickland, his wife, Mary Ann, and I were a part of a Peace Corps sent to help the Indians in a remote and mountainous area in Peru. My training was that of a psychiatric nurse, but often I functioned as the one to whom members of our group consulted in personal and confidential matters since I had taught catechism and counseled for years. Mary Ann in particular came to me with her problems and personal concerns.

One evening she came to my hut. It was obvious that she was very upset. We sat down. She told me about her, as she called it, "insane" and "frantic" fear of height. She did not realize how much she feared high places until we had moved into this country. Now she panicked every time she looked down or even thought about being on a mountain. Even when she closed her eyes, her hands began to perspire, and she felt panicky as she felt herself looking down from some height. She felt this fear was irrational; she did not know what caused it, but, she assured me, it was real. Even at night she would wake up and sit bolt upright in bed when she dreamed she was looking down from a high building or cliff. She had the feeling that she would fall and be destroyed. Several times she had awakened her husband with her behavior. He had told her to forget it and go back to sleep: "It must be something you ate that's giving you such nightmares." She knew, however, it was not food; she had this feeling every time she thought of being up high. "No one knows the agony I feel," she said, "when we have to ride in the bus up a narrow winding road to the top of one of the mountains." She continued, "I experience the same panic and fear when I have to ride the bus down the same mountain. I'm becoming a nervous wreck. I want to run and get out of this awful place. I don't know what to do — I know I shouldn't have such fears, but the fact is, I do."

If we had been in a city or in the United States, I would have sent Mary Ann to a clinician for therapy. It was clear to me from my training that this was a neurotic phobic reaction, but I did not know how to help Mary Ann, except to listen to her, as it were to "play it by ear."

Several times Mary Ann came to me, and I tried everything I knew to do, but with no results. I decided, finally, that one way might get her mind off her fears; have her turn her attention to something else. I had heard this had been done by having a person write his life story, perhaps only thirty minutes a day, but it helped. In addition it might give a clue to what was causing Mary Ann's problem. I did not pretend to be a professional therapist; I could do only what I thought best in the present situation where there were no clinicians available.

Mary Ann accepted the task I gave her. I told her to start with her earliest memories and write down everything she could remember. It seemed to relax Mary Ann somewhat, as she willingly began this new activity. I read what she brought me each time she visited me. I had no idea how to interpret, clinically, what she wrote and did not attempt to do so. Her story indicated her phobic fear of heights did not begin until about three or four years after her marriage. She did not recall being afraid of heights before, she said. One thing struck me; she never mentioned anything about sex, sex development, sexual activities, or emotional involvement with anyone. This was strange, since these are in integral part of everyone's life.

When Mary Ann finished her autobiography, I decided to confront her with the omission of anything related to sex in it. She excused herself by saying that her religious training was such that sex was never talked about; in fact, it was looked on as something rather evil, even if it were necessary for procreation. Clearly, she had an unhealthy attitude; if I was to serve as a counselor to her, it would be necessary for us to challenge her value system so that it could include a healthy and positive attitude toward human sexuality.

I said to her, "Mary Ann, I'm not trying to pry, but I think that not only your basic attitude toward sex needs to change, but also, to write an honest autobiography, you should include your sexual experiences."

Mary Ann seemed very upset. I assured her she did not have to write them down if she did not want to, only that her story was incomplete without them. She thought a moment and then coldly stated, "I think we have gone far enough into my personal life. What we have done hasn't seemed to help. Thank you for your efforts . . . but I think we should stop." With that, she left.

I did not see Mary Ann for some time; I assumed I had failed to be the counselor she needed. It turned out this was not accurate.

Two months after Mary Ann had decided to terminate our talks, she came to see me. She seemed somewhat embarrassed but, after a time began, "I was angry and scared when you talked the way you did to me about sex the last time I saw you. I decided, however, to write down my sexual experiences secretly." She paused. "As you know, I was brought up in a very strict puritanical family who never discussed sex and felt it was basically evil. For this and other reasons, I had no sexual experience until I was married — And, as I look back, I must have been a very poor sex partner for my husband. I let him feel I was performing the sexual act because it was my duty and the price I had to pay to have a husband and family. It must have been very unsatisfactory for him, particularly in view of the fact that he, too, had had little or no sexual experiences before marriage."

She paused and then continued, "I'm going to tell you something I've never told anyone. Two years after our marriage, I was alone with one of my husband's doctor colleagues. I don't know exactly what happened, but both of us became suddenly sexually excited, and for the first time I fully enjoyed sexual intercourse. After it was over I went home and was so stunned, I didn't know what to do, feel, or say. I hated to think I enjoyed it; it was contrary to everything that I had been taught and believed. Of one thing I was sure; I had committed the unforgiveable sin, and if I tried to enter heaven God would throw me down to hell." Mary Ann paused again. "That's when I began to be afraid of heights and falling. That's it — I haven't faced it — all these years I haven't wanted to face it because I have believed I cannot be forgiven and God is going to throw me into hell." Mary Ann became somewhat hysterical and it was necessary to wait for her to quiet herself.

An opportunity to be her spiritual counselor had come in an unexpected way. When she was more composed, we discussed her need to overcome these feelings of guilt. I asked her to go to her spiritual director, a member of our corps, and urged her to go to confession and obtain the forgiveness and absolution she needed.

I did not see Mary Ann for a few days. When she came to visit me, she seemed more composed. She now had faced what she had done and felt she had been forgiven in the eyes of God for it. She no longer felt she had committed an unforgiveable sin. It was now time for us to work together on a more realistic value system for the future, since her theology and moral value systems had been inadequate to help her face the traumatic effect of the sexual relations she had with her husband's friend.

After we came back to the United States, I did not hear from Mary Ann for many years. I did learn, however, she had lost her neurotic fear of heights and was a much more composed and self-assured woman than the one I had known in the Peace Corps.

Mr. Silks

As principal of a parochial high school, I had many duties. One was to be a pastoral counselor for the staff as well as for the students. I had taken a few courses in psychology during my seminary training, but I did not pretend to be a clinician. I always referred anyone needing therapy to a trained clinician. I was not able, however, to do so in the case of Mr. Silks.

Mr. Silks taught mathematics to the juniors and seniors. He was a brilliant man, but neither students nor staff members liked him. The students often complained that he was too strict.

"Gosh," one of them said, "he wants you to be perfect. You can't make a mistake or he jumps on you. Boy, you better not be even a minute late or he will really crawl your frame!" His classes got consistently lower grades than any others. The administration had a great deal of trouble explaining to parents and students alike why so many failed his courses.

Mr. Silks's relationship with the staff was equally bad. They knew that he often came to my office and to the assistant principal to point out some imperfection or mistake made in following the rules and regulations of the school. He would even report that a teacher took five minutes more for lunch than he was supposed to or one spent a great deal more time in the faculty lounge having coffee and gossiping with some other teacher instead of supervising the study hall.

From my point of view, Mr. Silks was a nuisance. He would check with me constantly to be sure he had followed, perfectly, the rules and regulations of the school. When I assured him he had done so, he seemed relieved, but in a day or so he was back in my office seeking reassurance and commendation.

I decided something had to be done about Mr. Silks. I knew he would not go to a clinician for help. However, I consulted Dr. Mowler, a clinical psychologist I knew. Dr. Mowler was very helpful. He informed me that he had known Mr. Silks all his life and that neurotic behavior we were witnessing was called, technically, *obsessive-compulsive behavior*. In layman's terms, Mr. Silks was a *perfectionist*. For the first time, I learned such perfectionism was an illness rather than a virtue. Dr. Mowler explained, "You see, perfectionists are in reality individuals who feel very inadequate and avoid insofar as possible making decisions for which they may be held responsible. They must live, as it were, in a rigid, structured box built of rules and regulations made by others. As long as they meticulously adhere to such dicta, they will not have to make a judgment and can avoid even moral responsibility for possible mistakes which would also expose their own fraility and inadequacy." Dr. Mowler added, "Don't be discouraged if he doesn't change. Even clinicians find it difficult and sometimes impossible to deal with persons who are obsessive-compulsive in their behavior.''

I went back better informed but with no plan to change the situation in the school regarding Mr. Silks. Reluctantly, I began to think it would be necessary to fire him for the good of the school. As it happened, events that followed made it unnecessary.

About two weeks after I saw Dr. Mowler, one of the other faculty members came to my office and said, "Did you know Mr. Silks has been late for class at least three times in the past week? I wonder what's up? Also, some of the students say they ask him questions in class and he seems not to be there. In fact, they couldn't believe him when he said they had been doing well enough so that there wouldn't be the usual six-week examination. All of us are wondering what's happened." I could offer no explanation. However, I was to share with Mr. Silks a short time thereafter what was a painful experience for him.

On Monday of the following week, Mr. Silks came to my office and announced he felt it was his duty to resign. I asked him why. At first he gave me no answer. Finally, in great pain he began: "This is strictly confidential." I nodded assent. He continued, "You know I have one daughter, Sylvia. She is now sixteen and a junior in our school."

I knew Sylvia, and she seemed such an unhappy girl. She was Mr. and Mrs. Silks's only child. I had heard how strict her father was with her, demanding the same perfection of her that he did of himself. She was never allowed to date or take part in the activities normal for her age and with her peers. Seldom did she smile or seem to be enjoying life. "Yes," I replied, "I know Sylvia very well."

It took some moments for Mr. Silks to continue. "Well . . . Sylvia is pregnant." As he said this, one could feel that Mr. Silks's entire world had crumbled and been destroyed. "I can't face the humiliation and shame of it. I don't know where I went wrong. I carefully guarded her and taught her to follow definite standards and to cherish certain moral and personal values. Now, all is gone."

I felt genuinely sorry for Mr. Silks; his pain was so intense and real. His rigid, structured box had been broken; it could never be the same again.

Although I felt badly for him, I recognized this as my opportunity to be a true pastoral counselor for him and his family. Our first duty was to Sylvia, as I saw it. I reminded him that when Our Lord was present at a gathering which intended to stone a woman caught in adultery, He reminded them, "He that is without sin among you let him first cast a stone at her." Since no one lifted a stone, He again said, "Neither do I condemn thee: go and sin no more." (John 8:7-11).

It was not the time to discuss Mr. Silks's own neurotic behavior but to help Sylvia. Mr. and Mrs. Silks and Sylvia and I worked together. It was decided in this particular case it would be better for Sylvia and Mrs. Silks to go to her grandparents' home in a distant state and immediately give the baby up for adoption as soon as it was born. Sylvia wanted it this way because she said she knew she could never really love the baby. She was confirming a saying that I had heard: "In most cases, a love child is never a loved child." (This was the right decision, as it proved to be in later years when Sylvia married a fine man and had three children. Her first child was placed in a home where he was welcomed and loved.)

Mr. Silks's entire personality changed during this time. He came out of his shell and in a real sense became human. The responsibility that was forced on him during Sylvia's pregnancy contributed to this change. He found that he was adequate and able to handle all contingencies. His changed attitude toward life was reflected in his classes and in his relationship with me and the rest of the faculty. He no longer was the perfectionist of old but a warm human being with whom peers and students alike could relate.

As his pastoral counselor, I spend many pleasant hours developing a theology and value system for Jim Silks that had meaning in the real world. It did not demand perfection but was concerned with human beings, with all their faults as well as their virtues. He slowly learned what a famous Jesuit had taught. The Scriptures say, "Man thou art dust and to dust thou shall return," but because of the Incarnation of Our Lord's love of mankind, one may add, "But dust thou art splendor."

Sister Theopolus

In addition to being the principal of a parochial high school, I was confessor and spiritual director for a convent of cloistered nuns. What I learned about obsessive-compulsive behavior and perfectionsim in the case of Mr. Silks was to be invaluable in dealing with a most painful form of neurotic obsessive-compulsive behavior known in religious circles as *scrupulosity*.

We had studied about scrupulosity in seminary. It occurred in some of the best-intentioned individuals, particularly nuns, monks, seminarians, and priests. Ironically, scrupulosity was most evident in those who sought to be perfect and to become saints. It involved rigid conformity to rules and regulations. In many cases, fraternal charity was abandoned in the mistaken and pharisaical attempts to follow rigidly the letter rather than spirt of an impossible rule of life. It was not comfortable to be with some of these would-be saints, especially when one recognized that he, himself, was an ordinary human being with faults who had made mistakes and fallen short of being perfect.

Thirty years ago, in my seminary days, we were taught to admire such heroic individuals in their efforts to become perfect. We were also taught that when it reached the point of scrupulosity — that is, a morbid and constant fear that one was sinning, regardless of how often one received absolution — the confessor should put the penitent under strict obedience to mind the confessor. The penitent was told to mind the confessor even when he or she was told not to come to confession except once a week and "you cannot commit sin in your present state of mind." Long since, many confessors have learned this attitude does not work. On the contrary, it may cause a complete nervous breakdown and emotional collapse. Only in recent years has it been recognized that scrupulosity is a special type of obsessive-compulsive neurotic behavior. It has nothing to do with piety or holiness: It is an illness.

With this knowledge, attitudes in pastoral care toward the scrupulous individual must change. He or she must be recognized as sick and in great pain. Like other obsessive-compulsive individuals, the scrupulous person feels inadequate and, above all, is afraid to make moral judgments for which he or she must be responsible. Hence, there is rigid conformity to a rule that makes it unnecessary for the individual to make judgments and assume moral responsibility for his or her behavior. Pastoral care for such an individual is difficult because of the rigidity of the scrupulous individual. I found this to be true in the case of Sister Theopolus.

Sister Theopolus was a nun in a cloistered convent. It was my intention to hear the sisters' confessions once a week at the most. However, this did not satisfy Sister Theopolus. Mother Superior would call me every day or two saying that Sister Theopolus wished me to come to the convent. Each time it was to go to confession for real or imagined infractions of some minor or petty rule. It became annoying when she repeated the same fault over and over again, seeking assurance that she had been forgiven. At times, I would suggest to her that her theology was weak, for Our Lord had said if she was truly sorry and contrite He would forgive her. In a sense, I told her, she was insulting Him when she came back with the same fault seeking reassurance of being forgiven. These preachments had no effect.

For many months I felt I was accomplishing little with Sister Theopolus, and being human, I found my contacts with her tedious and at times annoying. I simply prayed something would happen to change the situation. I hardly expected the change to come in the way it did.

One evening I was called to come immediately to the convent. Sister Theopolus had attempted to commit suicide. I hurried to the convent and for the first time entered the cloister proper. Sister Theopolus was lying in bed fully clothed in her religious habit with one addition: Several bandages were around her arms where she had tried to cut her wrists.

When I walked in she began to cry pathetically, "Oh, Father, I'm going to hell. . . . Now there is no help for me. I have committed the unforgiveable sin. I cannot be perfect. It is now impossible." I waited to be told about her "unforgiveable" sin — I knew of only one that Our Lord had declared unforgiveable, and that was final despair of His love and forgiveness.

After a few moments she confessed her "sin." "Father, I have
become more and more nervous in the past few months. The
harder I strived for perfection the more nervous I became, I read
our rules over and over again and tried in every way to live
them to perfection, but at times I would forget what I was
supposed to do or think in some situation when my book with
the rules in it was not with me. This made me feel worse and
worse. I began to lose sleep. In fact, some nights I didn't sleep
at all. It seemed like steam was building up in me and that I
was going to explode. Then, I did it. . . . I don't know why. I
released some of the tension I felt by committing an unforgiveable sin." She hesitated. "I masturbated — something that I
had never done before. I knew then I was lost, I could never be
perfect. I decided to end it all, but just as I began cutting my
wrists, it came to me that suicide was not the answer. I don't
know what to do. That is why I had Mother Superior call you."
She paused. "What can I do now?"

I informed her that she could begin to live a happy, holy,
and useful life. Her experience could be a turning point in a
positive direction in her personal and spiritual life. I assured
her that she had not committed the "unforgiveable sin"; she
had done what many others have done and are doing. I assured
her that masturbation had not hurt her health, nor would it
cause her mental problems. Above all, she could be forgiven.

After her confession, we began to talk. It was my opportunity
to begin as a pastoral counselor to help Sister Theopolus develop a more realistic value system and theology to include the
principles that she, like all humans, are not perfect and never
can be. God does not ask any of us to be perfect only to strive in
some ways toward perfection. Further, she needed to recognize
that God made us just as we are with our infirmities so that we
would turn to and cling to Him. If a human was perfect, he or
she might not seek God. I suggested that she meditate often on
the words of St. Paul: "Most gladly therefore will I rather glory
in my infirmities, that the power of Christ may rest upon me."
(2 Cor. 12.9) Sister Theopolus did not change overnight. It was
difficult for her to shed her scrupulous shackles, but in time her
confessions indicated that she had finally decided to join the

human race, and with God's help, strive to live a good, Christ-like life on earth with the hope and promise of eternal happiness in Heaven.

CHAPTER 7

DEPRESSION AND SUICIDE

THE alarming increase in depression and suicide in the last decade makes it mandatory that a pastoral counselor studies these emotional behaviors. What follows is a simple precursory overview of depression and suicide. It does not pretend to do more than alert the pastoral counselor to some of the more obvious signs and signals of the presence of neurotic or psychotic depressive reactions and potential suicide.

1. Mental health depends on the relationship of personality development, or *ego-strength,* and the relative intensity of stresses and strains on the human organism. An individual's mental health falls on a continuum from so-called healthy and normal through various stages of neurotic atypical feelings and behavior, when the stresses and strains are more than the personality can handle adequately, to psychotic manifestations, when the personality begins to disintegrate under extreme, unbearable pressure of self-destruction. Each person has his or her limits of tolerance for stress and strain. In wartime, for example, it was shown that even the best adjusted and strongest personalities had their breaking points, becoming psychotic in their behavior and often committing suicide under unbearable pressure.

2. *Depression* as a maladaptive and atypical emotion or feeling is to be distinguished from normal grief. If one's mother dies, it is natural to grieve. It is neurotic, however, to continue to grieve fifteen years later. If on the other hand, one is depressed and "grieves" when there is no reasonable cause for the grief or reacts to some distressing stress situation with more than the usual or appropriate amount of sadness and dejection, this, too, is neurotic and possibly psychotic depression. In this way, a pastoral counselor can easily judge whether the reaction of an individual is normal grief or is maladaptive depression. Where there is maladaptive depression, he or she needs, if pos-

sible, to refer the client immediately to a professional clinician, not only to therapeutically dissipate the depression but also to help the individual avoid potential suicide.

3. Suicide and those occurrences leading up to this act are essential knowledge for a pastoral counselor. However, even then the pastoral counselor may not be successful in preventing such an action. There are at least a minimal number of observations that may be made in suicide prevention and the care of potential suicidal individuals:

a. Always take seriously anyone's statement that they are going to commit suicide. When I was at the university, I was taught, "You can be sure that when someone comes right out and says he's going to commit suicide, he is not going to do so." Nothing could be farther from the truth. For example, a group of doctors were visiting one of their successful colleagues. He had an incurable cancer; however, he seemed jovial and had invited the group to his palatial home for dinner and refreshments. When all were upstairs in his sitting room telling jokes and having a convivial time, he said, apparently jokingly, "I'm going to kill myself." No one paid any attention to him. A few minutes later, they saw that their host had left the room. They heard a shot and rushed to the bedroom to find him dead. He had shot himself in the mouth and died instantly.

b. Many "suicides" are not really intended. These cannot be predicted unless an individual shows other signs of depression or atypical thinking, feeling, or behavior. The following story exemplifies this.

Mrs. McCally was a mother of seven children. Her husband drank far too much and could not keep a job. Mrs. McCally worked to support her children and took care of her husband when he was not "well." She seemed able to stand her situation until one day she learned that her husband was having an affair with another woman. Soon thereafter, Mrs. McCally was rushed to the hospital, her wrists slashed almost to the bone. I arrived at the hospital almost at the same time as the ambulance. I hurried to her room and she began to speak, almost hysterically, "Oh, Father, I don't want to die; I didn't intend to kill myself. I was only trying to get my husband Kenny's atten-

tion and maybe get him away from that other woman."
Unfortunately, it was too late. Four days later, I conducted her
funeral and burial service. To get attention is often the reason
individuals fake suicide. Unfortunately, they often succeed.
This is frequently the case with individuals who have alcohol
problems. In reality, it is a pathetic "cry for help." They did
not want to die; they really wanted someone to help them.

c. Deep depression and potential suicide is pathological.
Every effort should be made to get a depressed individual or
one contemplating suicide to a professional clinician, if it is at
all possible. When this is not possible, the pastoral counselor
or one serving as a counselor should seek to get the person to
talk. As long as he or she talks with the counselor, suicide is
less likely. It may involve literally hours of listening. Sometimes, through lengthy conversation, the potential suicide
victim becomes emotionally and physically so tired that he
rejects suicide for sleep; at other times, a motive to live becomes
evident and suicide is rejected.

d. Critically important for anyone dealing with a potential
suicide is an attempt in some way to discern whether *the will to
die is as strong or stronger than the will to live.* If it is, the
possibility of suicide becomes a probability. This becomes a
matter of relative values. For example, a woman has an incurable cancer and is in great pain. She weighs two alternatives: "Do I want to live with this pain, or would it be more
pleasant to be dead?" If she decides death has greater value,
suicide is a distinct possibility.

I could not help contrasting in this regard the attitude of two
women who had different value systems. Mrs. Fleming had
been a prominent socialite and hostess. At fifty years of age, she
had a bad fall and was told that she would never walk again.
She had cancer of the bone for which there was no known cure.
Three months later she killed herself. She preferred death to life
as an invalid. It was the opposite with Ming Toa. I saw her on
the isle of Molokai at the leper colony. Her eyes were empty
sockets; she had no feet, no hands, and no nose. She could not
leave her wheel chair, and yet, as I greeted her, a warm smile
traversed her emaciated face and mouth. I learned through an

interpreter that Ming Toa was a blessing to the hospital. Her cheerful acceptance of her condition did much for the other patients. Life meant something, even in her condition. She never considered death or suicide; her value system was different than that of Mrs. Fleming.

The most important assessment that can be made by any counselor when suicide is a possibility is this: "Does the individual consider death relatively more desirable than life?" If the answer is yes, suicide is definitely a possibility and every effort should be made to help the individual change his or her *thinking*. Without a change in thinking about the relative value of life over death, suicide is always a possibility. As the following cases reveal, a reason for living that was relatively more rewarding than the anticipated value in dying had to be found.

Peggy

As a part of my field experience before graduating and becoming a missionary, I chose to serve three nights a week on a hotline from midnight until 6 AM. We were told that many of the calls would be from teenagers who were homesick or high on drugs or alcohol or individuals who were lonely and simply needed someone to talk with them. We were also informed that once in a while someone might call who had a serious problem, even someone who was considering suicide. My first experience in such a case was Peggy, who called one morning at 2:30 AM.

I answered the telephone. A female voice began by saying, "I have a gun and I am going to kill myself. I simply called to tell you, since I don't have any friends or relatives where I live, that I'll be dead in a few minutes. I've left a note where my parents live so that you can make arrangements with them for the funeral."

The woman sounded so cool and determined her words sent a cold chill up my spine. What was I to do? I was not sure. However, I had been taught two things to do as a minimum in such cases: (1) to keep her talking as long as I could, and (2) during the conversation — no matter how long it took — to explore alternatives to live that might have relatively more influence on her than her desire to die. I consoled myself with the thought that at least she had called the hotline; perhaps, in reality, this was a final cry for help rather than a call to inform someone of her intention to kill herself.

At first, I told her I was glad she called and would be happy to talk with her. She began, "Don't try to talk me out of it, for I'm definitely going to shoot myself."

I said nothing for awhile. Finally, however, I said, "How can I know who you are if I don't know your name and take care of the arrangements if I don't know where you live?"

My questions seemed to make sense to her, for in a few minutes she began. "My name's Peggy. I'm twenty-three years old. I was brought up on a farm in Nebraska. A couple of years ago I got bored with farm life and came to the city. Boy, was that a mistake! I got a job waiting on tables in an all-night truck stop. You don't know how some of the jerks that come to such a place try to get to you. It's terrible. I could only afford this crummy room where I live; it's at 3850 Peach Street." She paused but then seemed to wish to continue; I did not stop her. "Well, I thought life was going to be great in the big city — well, it sure as hell is not. I haven't any girl friends and the men I meet are interested in only one thing." There was another long pause. Then she said, "Well, I finally met a fellow. I thought he was an all-right guy. I never had a boy-friend, and when he talked about marriage and kids and a home, I sure got to like him a lot." She stopped.

I was afraid she might quit talking and carry out her threat. I said, "Peggy, are you still with me?" I listened in silence for a seemingly endless time. Finally, from the other end of the phone I heard "Yeah" with a big sigh. "Well, tell me what happened."

She continued, "I don't like to think about it. . . . I really believed that guy, but, he really took me." Another long pause ensued. Finally, however, she continued, "Well, since we were going to get married and he wouldn't be back with his truck for a couple of weeks, I finally agreed to go to bed with him. I thought how great it was going to be — us two and maybe with our own baby, since I was just right for getting pregnant. The next morning he said, Thanks a lot, baby, I'll see you in a couple of weeks. It wasn't true. He didn't return for four months. I was pregnant. I thought he'd be glad to see me so I went up to him last night and said hello. He looked at me like he didn't know me and only said, Hey — What have I got to do with you? Get lost and don't bother me!" She began to cry and convulsively sob. I could only wait. She still had not carried out her threat, but at least she was still alive. When she partially composed herself she spent the next fifteen minutes repeating, "How could he do such a thing?" or "I haven't anyone — I'm a laughingstock — I want to die and get it over with."

During this time, which seemed like an eternity, I tried to think of something that might make her want to live rather than die. I suggested at first that her parents cared and would be hurt if she carried out her intention to commit suicide. This was ineffective. She informed me she had left home when her parents had urged her not to go and warned her of the potential dangers she would face.

Next, I suggested that she sounded like an intelligent woman. She was young and could have a happy life in spite of what had happened to her. This, too, was an unsuccessful approach. Equally ineffective was my appeal to any religious or moral values she might have. Her only answer was, "I let God down. He won't care what I do." I recognized that any attempt to show Peggy she was morally wrong would only aggravate and not alleviate the situation.

After thirty-five minutes, she and I were still talking. I was desperately trying to think of another approach. Without any thought of the possible success of one of my attempts, I suggested, almost incidentally, "Gosh, it sure is a shame that if you kill yourself; it won't be only suicide, but it will mean the death of a helpless little baby."

Peggy didn't say anything for a time. Then she said, "What did you say? Will you repeat what you said?" I again told her that killing herself would mean not only her death but also that of the baby within her. There was a pause, and then a painful cry from her: "Oh no, I don't want a little baby hurt. I love babies. No, I don't want the baby to die too."

All I could say was, "Peggy, you know that if you kill yourself, it will mean the death of the baby too."

I realized we were at a critical point in our relationship. It could go either way: life or death. After what seemed an interminable silence, Peggy said, "Could I come to see you — about the baby — I sure don't want anything to happen to it, no matter what happens to me." I assured her I would welcome meeting her and talking together.

In the weeks that followed, Peggy and I became close friends. Together, we developed a value system for her that made living more important than dying, particularly living for the baby. We talked of the baby and its future. We talked with her parents, who showed an understanding that neither of us could anticipate. It was agreed, with Peggy's consent, that her parents would raise the child on the farm and that she would work nearby. I had the pleasure of visiting Peggy's parents just before I graduated, two years after I first met Peggy. Tommy was the darling of his grandparents. In addition, Peggy was working in the small town nearby. She was looking forward to her marriage to Timothy, the owner of a small drygoods store. He knew the whole story and loved Peggy in such a way that it made no difference. Peggy found many satisfying reasons for living; suicide was out of the question.

Sam

Being a chaplain of a fire department in early 1930 was a trying experience. In late 1929, the stock market crashed. Hundreds of people were unemployed. Suicide by bankrupt financial tycoons was commonplace. The entire country was in a panic. New York City, the "money-capitol" of the world, was stunned. I was not surprised when I was called to help to prevent the suicide of a prominent head of one of the biggest stockbrokerage houses in America. I was surprised, however, when I arrived on the scene to see that it was my old friend, Samuel Levinson. He was standing precariously on the ledge of the tenth story of a Wall Street building. Several times he had threatened to jump, and all attempts to dissuade him had been of no avail. I had been called not only as a chaplain but a personal friend of Sam and his wife and family.

When I appeared on the scene, I was given a megaphone to talk to Sam. I was told that all of a sudden, he seemed to have gone berserk. He was at one minute sitting quietly at his desk; the next minute, screaming, he was out of the window of his office on the narrow precipitous ledge threatening that if anyone came near him he would jump.

In desperation, I had been called. I began by letting Sammy know who I was and begging him not to jump. His only answer was, "If you come near me, Denny, I'll jump." I assured him I would not touch him, but I would like to come up to the tenth story so I would not have to shout. Sam was ill, for he had always trusted me before; now, he seemed to doubt me. I repeated I would not touch him or do anything to stop him, except talk to him.

He finally let me come up, and a lengthy conversation followed as the police spotlights from below focused on Sam's every move.

My first approach to Sam was almost disastrous. I suggested that this would be a tragedy for his family. His reply was, "Why do you think I want to kill myself? All that I had planned and built up for my family is now gone. If I lived, I would have to sell the house, the cars, everything. I am completely broke. In fact, I owe debts I cannot pay. I can't face it. I have ruined my family and their future! It's because of what I have done to them that I want to end it all!" I tried a religious approach; it also did not work. "God is dead as far as I'm concerned," Sam said bitterly. This was not the Sam I had known, for he had been a very pious and religious man. Something, tragically, had happened to Sam's thinking.

For some time, I pleaded with Sam and tried to find a way to change his thinking. I seemed to get nowhere until we began to talk about his wife, Ruth. Together, they had started out without anything in a cheap flat in Brooklyn. They had worked hard and made many personal sacrifices to realize the

wealth and position they had before the crash. I could understand how painful it was to Sam to see all the things they had
worked for gone. However, Ruth meant more to Sam than
anyone or anything in the world. At one point, then, I said to
Sam, "And what do you think Ruth will feel and what will
happen to her if you are gone?" I paused. "Sam, I've known
both of you a long time. I knew you when you had nothing but
with Ruth by your side you made a success of both your lives.
What's going to happen to Ruth now? Don't you really love
her?" It was hard talk, but, for the first time in this long ordeal,
Sam seemed to calm down.

Almost wistfully, Sam began to reminisce. "Oh, those were
the days. Ruth and I lived in a cold-water flat. She did the
ironing, the cooking, the marketing, the housekeeping, but she
never complained. She worked hard. I did too. There were long
years of hard work, but we had great times working together
and raising our family. "Now," he said, "it's all gone . . .
nothing to show for all these years." He stopped; I was afraid,
at this point, he was going to jump.

Quickly, I tried to dissuade him: "But, Sammy, if you and
Ruth did it once, you can do it again. If you kill yourself, not
only have you become a quitter, but Ruth has had it!"

Sam was quiet for what seemed an eternity. Slowly, he said,
"No, no, I don't want anything to happen to Ruth. She is so
good. She's the most important thing in my life. No, nothing
must happen to Ruth!" The situation had reached a crisis.
Either he would jump to his death or find a reason for living,
he would choose to die or to find Ruth more important than
death.

Finally, I said, "Sam, let me call Ruth to come up here and
talk with you." Previously, he had refused. Now, slowly, he
said, "Okay."

Ruth hastened up to the office. Her first words were, "I love
you Sammy . . . I need you, don't leave me. We made it once —
we can do it again. I know we can make it. . . . What difference
does it make, as long as we have each other?"

Sam slowly entered his office. He looked pale and drawn. He
began to cry. All he could say was "Ruth . . . Ruth," as he

embraced her tenderly. My first duty as his counselor was over. However, later with Ruth's help, Sam and I examined his value system, which needed to be adapted to include values and goals other than monetary ones.

I said a prayer of thanksgiving as Sam and Ruth left the office. I also remembered the words of the Psalmist, "Out of the depths I have called unto you. . . . Lord hear my voice. (Ps 130)." He had heard all our prayers in this case.

Annabelle

Although I am a professional psychiatric social worker and took several courses in religion, psychology, and counseling at the university I attended while getting my master's degree, I know of no more difficult case in which I was involved, in my early years, than that of Annabelle Jones.

I met her when I was doing casework in the slums of Chicago. She was always dirty and unkempt. Her room was never cleaned and smelled of stale tobacco and rancid beer. I only visited her when she needed help in obtaining welfare checks and food stamps. She sat listlessly when I visited and said little. She seemed to live in a remote dream world that had only a tenuous connection with the real world.

Annabelle was a pathetic human being. She had been born in a small town in a modest, middle-class home. She was the only girl; she had one brother several years younger. Her father had deserted the family when she was a small child. Her mother worked but was unable to provide an adequate homelife for the children.

From her case history, I learned that Annabelle began smoking pot when she was eleven years of age and was expelled from the tenth grade for her frequent trips on acid (LSD). She did not seem to mind. She left home and came to Chicago. The record further revealed that, after awhile, she had so many "bad trips" from acid that she switched to alcohol and soon became an addict. From then on, she lived with any man who would provide her with pot and booze. Unfortunately, when she drank too much she would have what is known as *flashbacks,* reliving some of her bad trips. During such flashbacks she ran up and down the stairs of the apartment building, screaming and shouting obscenities and scantily clad. No man remained with her very long because of her behavior; many people feared that she might kill herself or them during these outbreaks.

On one occasion, the police were called when she was found lying in a drunken stupor on the sidewalk outside the apartment. When they tried to take her away she began screaming, swinging her fists at the police, and attempting to bite them. Because of her actions, she was taken to a mental institution for observation and treatment.

In the hospital, without her marijuana and alcohol, she became shy, withdrawn, and in a constant state of depression. Stimulants were administered, but most of them caused a manic reaction. This, in turn, required the use of tranquilizers. It soon became clear that she could easily become addicted to some of these, particularly Demerol®.

Annabelle stayed about ten months in the institution and was released. For two months, she held a job in a department store, but then the drinking began again with the pot and acid flashbacks. When she could, she lived with any man who would supply her addictive needs. A time came when she had no one. This was the time she applied for welfare and I met Annabelle for the first time. I felt badly for Annabelle, but at that time, she was almost unapproachable. Only a series of traumatic events brought us closer together.

I received an unexpected call from the general hospital and was surprised to hear that Annabelle had asked for me. Three days before, while drinking, Annabelle had one of her worst flashbacks. A neighbor reported that she was seen running and screaming up and down the steps of the three-story apartment house. She must have done so twenty or thirty times at about 1 AM. She knocked on the neighbor's door. When the frightened neighbor refused to answer the door, Annabelle literally broke the door with her body and entered screaming, "The devil's after me. I can't hide. Look outdoors. Those are not really trees. See, they are moving. They are all the devil's agents after me. They are coming to get me. I can't run fast enough. I can't get away." She stopped for a moment, and then with glazed eyes and a curious smirk on her lips, she continued, "I know what I'll do. I'll join them. Yes, that's what I'll do, and then they can't get me." She began to giggle, "I'll fool them; I'm going to die, and then they can't get me anymore."

With that, she rushed back to her room, took all the phenobarbital she had in the bottle, staggered down the stairs, and collapsed in the street. She was rushed to the hospital. She was in serious condition, but fortunately, she did not have enough phenobarbital to kill her. As soon as she was better, she demanded that she be given Demerol and certain other tranquilizers. When the hospital authorities refused, she became angry and declared, "If you don't give me some, I will jump out of the window." She meant business; an orderly passing by her room saw her trying to raise the window with the obvious intention of jumping out. The staff decided to transfer her to the psychiatric ward in the hospital. Shortly thereafter, I was asked to come to the hospital.

I was informed that Annabelle had asked that they contact me. I could not understand why until she told me herself. When I entered her room without any greeting, she began, "I had them call you because I'm at the end of my rope. I'd rather die than live. I'm tired of living. I just want some rest. I look forward to the peace I'll know when I'm dead. I'm tired of being sick and of this rat race called living." She paused, then continued, "Maybe you wonder why I had them call you. Well, you see, I wanted at least one person to know what I was going to do. I couldn't think of anyone but you. I don't have any friends or anyone close. I thought somebody should know, so I decided it would be you."

Although it seemed that Annabelle was determined to take her own life, it was possible she could be dissuaded and that contacting me was a small cry for help and understanding. I said to myself, "How can I help?" Annabelle's value system did not go beyond that of a "high," a "drunk" or the life of a prostitute. It was difficult to know where to start if one were to help Annabelle change her thinking so that life and living would be accepted as preferable to the peace she expected for her tormented soul by dying.

All that I could think to say was, "Annabelle, do me one favor. Don't do it until you and I can get better acquainted. I won't stop you, but you don't need to rush it. I'd like it if you would wait awhile."

Annabelle looked at me in surprise and amazement, then commented, "Well, I'll be damned. I didn't think anyone would want to hear anything about me and my rotten life. You must be nuts, or kidding me . . . are you on the level?" I assured her I was. "Okay," she answered, "but don't say I didn't warn you. What you're going to hear will make your hair curl. It's not a pretty story: In fact, it's downright rotten." With that, I left to return in two days.

Several visits produced little upon which to build. Her value system was devoid of anything positive or energizing. It was little wonder that she considered death a relatively more valuable potential state than her present life situation. I was convinced, however, that something could be found that would make living more attractive to her than death. I decided on a technique for counseling that I had used in certain other cases. I asked Annabelle to do some writing for me each day. I assured her I did not care about how she wrote. I knew that her education had been limited; I did not expect good grammar or sentences. I simply wanted her to put down, in her own way, certain memories.

Her first task was to write down the things in her past that she remembered as pleasant and happy. Later, I asked her to write down things she liked and liked to do that made her happy. We had agreed she would not include the euphoria induced through the use of drugs, alcohol, or the like. Finally, I asked her to pretend and dream that she could be anything she would like and have anything in life she wanted. When I assigned her this final task she sighed and said, "That's easy. I wish I was the happy little girl I used to be and had the fun I had as a child. That is the time before I began smoking pot and getting into trouble."

I was not surprised when she made this statement. Everything she wrote suggested she had been a happy child. In her own mind, she contrasted the pleasures and joys she knew then with her present ugly and intolerable life.

One day, I said something that startled Annabelle. After I had let her reminisce pleasantly for fifteen or twenty minutes about her childhood, I said, "Annabelle, you know you'd be terrific working with girls and helping them avoid the mistakes you feel you've made." She looked at me in amazement. She asked me to repeat what I had just said. I repeated, "With your experience, you could help a lot of young women avoid the same behavior that you now feel is rotten and no-good. Just think what it would mean if you could help young girls stay out of the kind of trouble you've gotten in. No one could tell them better — from experience — what you could."

Annabelle looked at me and after a few moments shook her head in disbelief. "You're kidding me or pulling my leg, aren't you?" I shook my head to indicate I was not. After awhile she continued, "Do you really mean you think I could help a bunch of kids? You must be nuts. No one would want my help."

I was prepared for her last remark. "Oh, yes, I know the very place you could be useful, and I can get you a job there." I then explained to her about a new experimental program being sponsored by the state for delinquent and homeless girls. Instead of living in large dormitories as they might do in an orphanage or reformatory, twenty girls were assigned to a pleasant cottage. A trained counselor served as housemother. In addition, a cook and a housekeeper lived in the cottage. There was an opening for a housekeeper in one of the units. I knew I could get Annabelle the job of housekeeper if she was willing to accept the position.

At first, Annabelle laughed at the suggestion: "Imagine me teaching girls how to keep clean and keep their rooms clean. You've been to my flat. It wasn't the best kept place you've been in, was it?" I had to agree, but I assured her that she could change and that her unkempt flat, in all probability, reflected her true feelings about herself and the life she had been living.

"Well, I'm game; I'm willing to try anything I haven't already tried. But, don't be disappointed if I fail; that's the story of my life."

A new life began for Annabelle. The adjustment was difficult at first, but she quickly began to take an interest in the girls. In turn, almost as if by instinct, they turned to her for advice and help. Although not very articulate, Annabelle was able to teach the girls in a practical and down-to-earth way a great deal about life and the problems young women face in the outside world. Slowly, Annabelle developed a new value system, and living "with and for her girls," as she put it, made suicide out of the question: "I'm too busy right now to think about dying — maybe later — but not right now. I got too many things to do."

Paul

As Paul's pastor, I had taken several courses in counseling in the seminary and enjoyed working as a pastoral counselor. It was natural for Paul to come to see me when he was asked to leave the religious order he wished to join. Knowing Paul well, I intended to be supportive and sympathetic but would avoid letting Paul become too dependent on me for decisions and to avoid personal responsibility.

Paul and I spent an hour together two days after he returned home. He was now twenty-two years of age, tall, slight young man. When he entered my office, he quickly began to tell me his story. "Father, I had to see you as soon as possible, for I've had the craziest urge to kill myself. I try not to think about it, but it keeps coming back. I'm even afraid to walk to the top of the hill. I have a feeling that I will jump into the canyon. I know it's irrational, but that's how I feel."

Although I used a nondirective method of counseling, for brevity's sake, I shall indicate only what came out of the various counseling sessions.

Paul had always wanted to be a priest, and it was taken for granted that he would become one by his parents. Paul had decided on entering a religious order rather than becoming a secular priest. After eighth grade, he entered the community and attended the high school run by the fathers and brothers.

He did well during his high school days and the two years of philosophy, as the first two years of college are called. He would soon enter major seminary, the equivalent of four years of graduate school in a secular college. However, in this particular community, the year before going to major seminary was spent as a novitiate, in what was intended to be "spiritual formation." There were no formal classes, and the time was spent in spiritual exercises and reading and additional time in prayer and meditation and gradually developing those virtues considered necessary for the religious life. This time of formation had inestimable value for most candidates for community life. In a few cases, however, the admonitions to "seek perfection" became a source of anxiety and concern. These existed for those who tended to be neurotically obsessive-compulsive, perfectionists, and scrupulous. Unfortunately, Paul was a perfectionist and became more and more scrupulous. It was easy to understand how these emotions and behavior developed. His parents had expected, and still expected, Paul to be perfect. That is, he was not allowed to be a human being but was expected to be the family's saint who could and would do no wrong.

Paul explained, painfully, how he looked forward to returning to the cloister and his community after a short visit home. Unfortunately, upon returning, he soon became depressed, listless, and despondent. He simply could not be the perfect saint he wanted and was expected to be. No matter how hard he tried, he felt he could not be perfect. "Why," as he explained, "I fall asleep every morning, or nearly every morning, when I'm supposed to be meditating." (I recalled I had done the same thing, since meditation was at 4:30 AM.) The more he thought about his imperfections, the more depressed he became, and the more depressed he became, the less attentive he was to his simple duties and the house rules and regulations.

The final blow came when Paul began to masturbate. He was sure he was going to hell and would be damned. His confessor was no help and even suggested that his developing habit was a definite indication that Paul did not have a religious vocation (an attitude considered scientifically indefensible and ridiculous by most spiritual directors and confessors today).

Because of Paul's behavior, the superiors of the community asked Paul to leave; they did not feel he belonged in religious life.

Paul's family was crushed. When Paul saw his family's reaction to his dismissal, he became deeply disturbed and considered suicide as a possible way out of his situation.

My role as pastoral counselor was twofold. First, I would help Paul with both his irrational and rational guilt, particularly regarding masturbation. Second, it was my duty to help Paul expand and modify his value system to include a realistic attitude toward fallible humans, including himself, and to learn that a vocation other than that of a religious could be rewarding and sustaining.

In regard to masturbation, I could assure him that there was no danger of physical deterioration or harm. I further indicated that there need not be any psychological anxiety or damage from masturbation. Only guilt feelings and inner conflicts that were not handled could cause a problem. Thus, it would not be the masturbation as such that might cause psychological problems but feelings of guilt that were not resolved, producing anxiety and tension.

I assured him that many individuals developed this habit to achieve a kind of physical and psychological relief, rather than for sexual excitation and gratification, and I felt this was true in his case.

It was useful to point out a teaching of the church that Paul had learned in seminary. Habits tend to weaken one's ability to make free choices, and when acts are performed without sufficient freedom of choice, culpability is lessened and a reason for moral guilt may not exist at all.

Together, Paul and I worked on his problem. After awhile, he took a less anxious attitude toward his habit. He never felt, in his own conscience, that masturbation was entirely morally acceptable. For that reason, he mentioned it in his monthly confessions. However, he did not feel it necessary to run to confession every day after he had masturbated.

It was vitally important for Paul's mental and spiritual

health that he overcome his perfectionistic attitude toward himself and others. This was one of the most difficult aspects of our counseling relationship, for it involved the real cause for it: Paul's personal feeling of inadequacy and inability to accept moral responsibility for his own behavior. In time, however, he was able to accept himself as another fallible human being who could not, even if he tried, be an impeccable god.

Exploring Paul's value system, his interests, and his likes and dislikes was a pleasant experience for both of us. Paul was a brilliant, sensitive young man. He was artistically inclined and showed a marked interest in other people and their welfare. In time, Paul understood that the priesthood and the religious life were not the only ways to serve God. There were many alternative ways to achieve the same end. Together, we discovered that Paul enjoyed studying psychology, as he admitted, "even more than studying philosophy and theology." We finally agreed that Paul should enter a university and study psychology.

Paul worked hard at the school. With financial help from home and an evening job in a restaurant, he was able to pay his way through undergraduate school. Afterward, because his grades were so good, he was offered a position as a graduate assistant in the psychology department. He obtained his master's degree and, finally, his doctorate in clinical psychology.

Paul loved to work with young people. Therefore, he accepted a position in the student guidance and counseling center in a large university. Paul never married; his work was his entire life. From all reports, he became an excellent counselor and therapist. Further, his seminary training had prepared him to serve as a competent pastoral counselor for many students.

When I visited Paul in his office one day, I was pleased that he never ceased to remind himself that he was human and needed, at all times, to be honest with himself both in the assessment of his weakness and strengths and of his abilities and shortcomings. On the plaque on the wall behind his desk were inscribed the famous words of advice given by Polonius to his son, Laertes, in Shakespeare's *Hamlet* (act 1, scene 3): "This above all. To thine own self be true, and it must follow as the night the day, thou canst not then be false to any man."

Part IV
Atypical Acting out and
Antisocial Behavior

CHAPTER 8

ATYPICAL ACTING OUT AND ANTISOCIAL BEHAVIOR

BY far the largest group of individuals who come to the counselor are those whose actions are a source of concern and are often, disruptive to families, friends, and society in general. Although these cases are the most numerous, unfortunately individuals with these behavior problems seem to be the most resistant to counseling. There are several reasons for this resistance and difficulty in counseling, which the pastoral counselor needs to know. Three principle causes for this resistance are present in many instances: lack of motivation, faulty personality development and the self-concept, and maladaptive use of defense mechanisms.

Lack of Motivation

Unfortunately, many individuals resist change even when their actions are dangerous to themselves or to others or both. Change is one of the most frightening experiences for most human beings, even change in the manner in which one acts and behaves. This seems particularly true in the case of individuals whose actions are atypical. In many cases, an individual must hit a painful bottom — must hurt enough — to want and be willing to change. For example, the person with an alcohol problem may have to lose health, home, a job, or all three before he or she is motivated to seek help and to change. Often, the individual waits too long and death, rather than change, results.

Certain cases illustrate the resistance to change that is possible and the pain necessary to prompt an individual to seek counseling and to attempt to change.

Carl had been sent to several treatment centers for his problem with alcohol, but he showed little interest or desire to

99

change his habits, even though he admitted that he often had blackouts when drinking; he could not remember where he was or what he was doing many times while drinking. He was now thirty-one years of age and had been drinking excessively for at least ten years. Attempts by family and friends urging him to change his behavior and seek help were to no avail. Only when he hit a painful and tragic bottom was he motivated to stop drinking. He and two of his drinking associates became intoxicated. They went to the home of Carl's girl friend. That is the last he remembered. Sometime later he was found sitting in the rain with a woman's purse in his hands. The police noted the woman's name and address, which was contained in the purse. With Carl, they returned to the woman's apartment to find her hanging dead from an improvised rope made of a bed sheet. The police then sought the other two men: One was found dead where he had fallen into an excavation while intoxicated, and the other turned state's evidence on Carl. Carl was tried, sentenced to prison, and had been there for over four years. Tragically, he told the pastoral counselor at the prison, he was in blackout and honestly did not know if he had committed the crime. Carl resolved never to drink again and to seek help for his addiction upon his release from prison.

Selma began to use drugs when she was fifteen and became addicted to them. Often she resorted to stealing to get the money to satisfy her addictive habit. Many times she was placed in jail for stealing and for prostitution. For seventeen years after she began using drugs, she showed no willingness to change her behavior. It was not until she was thirty-two years of age that she became motivated to change her life-style. She came tearfully at that time to her friend, a nurse, for pastoral counseling. She had just learned that, because of her prostitution, she now had an advanced stage of a veneral disease that could cause permanent damage to her brain if not treated. She resolved to give up prostitution and drugs immediately.

Howard was a young man of twenty-three when seen by the counselor. His early life and family background seemed to have destroyed any and all feeling in him for other people and their property. His father had a serious problem with alcohol. When drunk his father often beat him and his mother. He was forced to go to work at an early age as an unskilled laborer. Howard was constantly in trouble with the law for fighting, stealing, and destroying property. Even having been in jail many times did not motivate Howard to change his behavior. The turning point for him came in a nearly tragic way. Many times he had injured poeple when he would knock them down to steal their money. However, it was only after a serious incident that he sought counseling. He pushed an elderly woman to the ground with the intention of stealing her purse. Her head struck the concrete curb and she was knocked unconscious. She was rushed to the hospital, and it was a serious question whether she would live. It was not until Howard realized the possible consequences of his behavior that he decided he must change his behavior. Fortunately the woman recovered and refused to press charges. Shortly thereafter, Howard joined the Marines. After that, his fighting was confined to protection of the innocent and as a Marine Officer.

Marian came to a counselor when she was twenty-eight years of age. Her husband had just left her for another woman. In the course of the counseling sessions, she admitted she had been spoiled by her mother, and she had never really grown up but had remained immature and childish. She demanded the same treatment from her husband as her mother had given her. It took the breakup of her marriage for her to realize that she had to change. Unfortunately, it was too late to save her marriage, but it was possible through counseling to help Marian to a more mature life-style.

Many times, even professional therapists and counselors are tempted to terminate the therapeutic or counseling relationship when there seems to be no way to motivate clients to change behavior. However, counselors should not be discouraged but accept empirically the unfortunate and often frustrating fact that not even the most skilled and highly trained professional can do anything for a patient or client until the individual wants help and is willing to accept the help of the counselor. The pastoral counselor, like other counselors, can do nothing for a client until he or she is ready, except pray for the individual, patiently wait, and be available if the client decides he or she needs to change his behavior and wants help to accomplish this change. Such waiting may be painful for the counselor. Often he can do nothing but wait, watch, and pray that the individual does not destroy himself or others before he resolves to change. It is painful, for example, for a counselor of individuals with alcohol problems to stand by helplessly while he watches many of these potential clients destory themselves and even reject help and die.

Motivation and attempts to motivate are essential and integral aspects of the counseling process. Two things are important as possible motivators: (1) when the pain, hurt, and misery within the individual becomes so great that the person wants and seeks to change and (2) when the individual recognizes the potential or actual, serious consequences that may follow from his actions. The counselor can do little about pain within an individual as a motivator; however, it is possible that the counselor can help the client recognize and understand the potential consequences to himself and others if the negative behavior continues. It follows, therefore, that the primary role of the counselor in regard to motivation is to help the client realistically, in terms of his or her value system, to assess the possible disastrous consequences if the behavior is not changed or eliminated entirely.

Faulty Personality Development and the Self-Concept

The chief reasons for resistance to change in many cases are basically the personal feelings of inadequacy and poor self-concepts of the individuals who need help. In many instances, a healthy self-concept and self-esteem never developed; in other cases, antecedent poor self-concepts are undermined and feelings of inadequacy further aggravated because of alcohol or drug dependency, incarceration, poverty, or other circumstances or conditions.

An adequate self-concept never developed in a man of thirty, who acted like a teenager. He had become bitter, resentful, and hostile because he was required to work and could not go to high school and enjoy the normal activities of more fortunate youths. He felt cheated of his adolescence and, as a result, continued to act out his need for adolescent gratifications as a grown man.

A woman of thirty-five was creating daily turmoil and confusion in her home and with her husband and family. It was found, in her case, when her background was studied, that she had a very cold mother who paid little attention to her as a child. As a result, the woman did not develop a normal feeling of self-respect and self-esteem. She found, however, during her childhood that the one way to get the attention of her mother from whom she wanted love was by negative behavior, such as throwing tantrums, screaming, and misbehaving in general. When she misbehaved, her mother paid attention to her, thus rewarding the negative behavior of her daughter. From her childhood on, the woman lived by the conviction that to get the attention one wants from a loved one is by negative behavior. Her immature and childish standards existed because a mature self-concept and personality never developed.

On the other hand, there are individuals who may have inadequate self-concepts that are further weakened when the person becomes dependent on drugs or alcohol or for other reasons. For example, Thelma was born in the ghetto and lived in poverty in the street. Development of an adequate personality structure and healthy self-concept was impossible. Her father had disappeared and her mother made her living as a prostitute. Many times as a child and teenager, she would come home to their one-room flat and find her mother and a strange man in bed together. In her fourteenth year, she began to turn to drugs. She, too, became a prostitute to obtain the money for her drug habit. By the time she was eighteen she had been in jail six times and a women's reformatory once for two months. Finally, when drugs were taken away from her she, disgusted with herself and her society, attempted suicide. Through the use of drugs and prostitution, her poor self-concept disintegrated even further to the point that she felt life was not worth living. Happily, she found help for her drug problem in a home with others who also had drug problems. She found she was not the only person with a poor self-concept and drug dependency. With mature counseling, she was able after a year of rehabilitation to begin a new life for herself in a new environment.

The pastoral counselor should not attempt to analyze or treat the underlying problems that cause poor self-concepts and feelings of inadequacy. This is the special role and function of a trained clinician. The counselor must recognize, however, that in many cases there has been faulty personality development, leaving the individual with an inadequate self-concept.

In the course of counseling, the conversation and the behavior of the client often reveals the area or areas in which the person feels inadequate and those related to a poor self-concept. The counselor may wish to evaluate the client's inadequacy in terms of possible answers to the following five sets of questions.

1. Does the client act immature, or is the client's behavior and conversation appropriate to his or her chronological age and education?
2. Does the person indicate that he or she feels socially unacceptable or personally worthless?
3. Does the individual appear to be overly dependent on some other person or persons?
4. Does the individual accept the fact that he or she is a fallible human being who is worthwhile, regardless of mistakes, failures, or past behavior? Is the person intolerant of himself or herself because of failures to achieve certain goals or live up to what may be impossible, perfectionistic standards? Are the goals of the individual realistic? Are they too high or too low?
5. Does the person appear to have low tolerance for the everyday stresses and strains that are to be expected in every human life?

Although it is not the role of the pastoral counselor to analyze or to treat the basic personality problems of any individual, he has a significant pastoral role to play in helping an individual improve his or her self-esteem, self-confidence, feeling of personal worth, and self-concept. This can be done only as the counselor assists the client to separate *person* from *behavior* and to see that no matter what thoughts, words, deeds, or omissions in the past are unacceptable, the person is still to be honored, respected, and loved by him- or herself. Further, the client should realize the honor and respect one desires from others cannot be achieved until one first loves, respects, and honors himself as a unique person.

One of the most difficult but important tasks of a pastoral counselor is to guide a client in gaining self-esteem and self-respect. Many methods and techniques have been used by counselors in their attempts to help clients achieve self-confidence and a feeling of personal worth. The most important assistance to the client is in an indirect manner; the counselor projects to the client not only the respect the counselor has for the client but the respect the counselor has for him- or herself. It is a truism, but a valid one, that a person cannot give what he or she does not have. Unless the counselor respects himself, he cannot assist a client to self-esteem and self-respect. Both counselor and client do well to remind themselves of their personal worth. The Psalmist reminds all men, "What is man [O Lord], that thou art mindful of him? and the son of man that thou visitest him? For thou hast made him a little lower than the angels, and has crowned him with glory and honor." (Ps. 8:4-5)

Maladaptive Use of Defense Mechanisms

As noted earlier, defense mechanisms are considered to be means used by human beings in attempts to dissipate and eliminate the tension arising from anxiety because of frustrations, conflicts, pressures, and other stresses and strains. Through the use of adaptive mechanisms, all or most of the tension, pressure, and anxiety may be eliminated. Further, through the use of so-called semiadaptive mechanisms, an individual is able to handle at least part of the anxiety caused within the human organism. However, there are many maladaptive defense mechanisms that erroneously lead an individual to believe the tension and anxiety has been released. In reality the psychological pressure or "steam" known as anxiety still remains in the organism and may cause serious problems, harm to the human being, and possibly physical or mental illness.

Of the many maladaptive defense mechanisms used by human beings, at least three are used frequently by individuals who display maladaptive acting out and behavior problems. These are called (1) *rationalization,* (2) *intellectualization,* and (3) *denial.*

1. When someone rationalizes, he or she decides intellectually that there is a good and legitimate reason for an action. In reality, there is no such reason. A person, for example, with an alcohol problem can find dozens of reasons for taking a first drink. The person is too hot or too cold, too fat or too slim, too high or too low. It does not matter: Many reasons, often contradictory, are found to intellectually justify taking that first drink. A drink, however, in the case of the alcohol addict, leads to progressively more drinks and eventually to intoxication.

2. Intellectualization is another frequently used defense mechanism. When a person rationalizes, he or she finds intellectually what appears to be a logical reason for performing an action; when he convinces himself he cannot help acting as he does, he is intellectualizing. He may say to himself, for example, "It seems to be that it is one of the curses we must suffer in my family, since most of the men develop alcohol problems." Or, he may say, "Like others, I must fight for my race against other races, or I will lose my personal identity." Or, again, "I'm subject to migraine headaches and the only thing that eases them are these tranquilizers." (The tranquilizers were not prescribed by the physician, who would have given the person a non-addictive medication.) Intellectualization is used by an individual to help alleviate the person's feeling of guilt for maladaptive behavior and to insulate the person from the emotional impact and guilt that might be felt. If one can say, "I act this way because I can't help it," one may feel less culpable for actions that may be antisocial or destructive to oneself or others.

3. Denial is an intellectual mechanism used by a person in an effort to convince himself that he does not have a problem. A person with an alcohol problem may have been in jail many times, been fired from many jobs, lost his family, and destroyed

his own health but may still maintain that he has no problem related to alcohol. A naive listener may assume, erroneously, that the person is deliberately lying to cover over his addictive problem. This is not necessarily true. It is more likely that he has convinced himself intellectually that he really does not have a problem. He reasons that he could handle the problem except for some insurmountable obstacle. He could handle the problem but for some reason. The "but" has led the person to lie to himself. He has said to himself, "I could handle alcohol, *but* I need it to relieve my tensions." "I could handle it *but* for my wife, *but* for my boss, *but* for my job, *but* for . . ."

When all three of these defense mechanisms are used by a drug or alcohol addict, the resistance to treatment may be great. One may hear the addict saying to himslef, "I need a drink or I will get violently ill" (rationalization). "Besides, I can't help drinking heavily, it seems to run in the family" (intellectualization). "However, I don't really think I have a problem. I could handle alcohol, but I have a nervous condition that requires that I drink to control it" (denial).

It is not important for the pastoral counselor to define the defense mechanisms used by clients. However, it is important for the counselor to understand that when clients use mechanisms to defend their behavior they may not be lying deliberately. Instead, the individual may be using these mechanisms to justify continued maladaptive behavior that he believes he cannot control and that he considers a hopeless condition. The counselor can help such a client by indicating not only that both should look realistically at the facts but also that control is possible if the real condition can be admitted and accepted honestly. More important, the counselor should realize the client has sufficient confidence in himself that he can change his behavior.

One of the most effective counseling techniques involves a mutual examination of the value system of the client in terms of what she or he is paying for the gratification that comes from the addictive or maladaptive behavior. Both may ask, "What is the young woman paying in terms of health by using drugs; what is she getting as a reward instead? It is worth it?"

One with an alcohol addiction might ask himself the following questions: "What is alcohol giving me as a reward to compensate for the loss of my wife and children?" "Is it worth spending years in prison in order to continue my antisocial, rebellious, hostile, and belligerent behavior?" "What am I willing to pay in terms of my marital life and conjugal happiness so that I can continue being immature, selfish, and having my own way?"

It should be reassuring to a counselor to find that clients usually welcome honesty from the counselor and the opportunity to be honest with themselves. The client, in most cases, respects the counselor who accepts him as a worthwhile person with a problem not condoning his or her behavior or accepting his attempts intellectually to justify abhorrent behavior. The counselor is successful if he can help the client not only improve his or her feeling of self-confidence, self-esteem, and self-worth but also can help him or her develop a more rewarding value system. This involves a realistic assessment of what the client is willing to pay for a more rewarding life-style and what it may cost ultimately if the client continues his or her present destructive and enervating behavior. The ultimate question is, "For what shall it profit a man, if he shall gain the whole world, and lose his own soul?" (Mark 8:36)

Addictions

Because addictions involve not only problems of personality development but also physiological problems of drug, alcohol, or other dependency, they warrant a brief special consideration.

Alcohol and other drug dependencies are epidemic in the United State and are rapidly becoming the same in many countries throughout the world. Because of this, it is important for the pastoral counselor to study addictions as much as time and opportunity permits. Here, only a brief sketch and outline of a few important points for the counselor to consider regarding addictions are presented.

1. The question of what is meant by *addiction* is debated by experts throughout the world. There is no universal agreement.

Some students believe that alcoholism and drug dependency are symptomatic of much deeper personality disorders that should be given priority in treatment; others feel that alcoholism and other drug dependencies are primarily and almost exclusively physical and physiological problems. The pastoral counselor does not concern himself with this question; it does not affect his or her specific role as counselor.

Before 1935, alcohol addiction was viewed in progressively different ways; to some degree, other addictions were viewed in a similar way. Less than two centuries ago, the "town drunk" was accepted and nothing made of drinking. Even in recent years, movies played up inebriation as comedy material. With the evolution of Protestant puritanism and Catholic Jansenism, alcoholism was gradually considered sinful and the addict considered a "moral degenerate." Shortly thereafter, with the ascendency of Freudian psychoanalysis as a major influence in the field of physical and mental health, the person with an alcoholic problem was labeled as "mentally ill." Finally, with Prohibition, he was considered a "criminal," or worse. Regrettably, too many, even today, treat an individual who has an alcohol or drug problem as morally degenerate, mentally ill, or criminal. It was not until recent years, largely through the dedicated efforts of many who associated themselves with Alcoholics Anonymous, the *disease concept* of alcoholism began to be accepted and championed in scientific and other professional fields. This was a giant step forward for the addict, since it meant that treatment and rehabilitation, not incarceration, was the proper way to handle those who were alcohol or drug dependent.

Unfortunately, the disease concept had certain inherent shortcomings, which have lead to some misunderstandings. The average layman can understand what is meant by *acute* or *subacute* illnesses such as pneumonia or measles, which he understands are often curable. Further, he can understand the concept of *chronic* illness, such as heart disease or circulatory dysfunction. He accepts the fact that these are usually not able to be cured but can be treated for control purposes. Addiction, however, as a form of disease, is not able to be fitted into these categories. It shares, in common with chronic illnesses, the notion that addictions cannot be cured and, at best, can be controlled, but it is essentially quite different from chronic disease as it is popularly understood.

There are many sophisticated and complicated definitions of addictions. These need not concern the counselor. A simple and pragmatic definition, however, suffices and indicates the basic difference between addiction and other disease entities. *One is addicted to something when he or she has lost the freedom to use the substance adaptively or in a healthy, useful way.* For example, the person addictively dependent on alcohol has no problem until the first drink is taken. Such a drink triggers a condition that is thought to be in the nervous system of the individual, creating, at least, a psychological need and compulsion to have another drink, then another, and then another, until intoxication results.

There are many things to which one can become addicted: alcohol, drugs, candy, and food. One drink leads to many more for the person with an alcohol problem; for the obese person, one piece of candy leads to eating the whole box. Both are addictions; however, one is more socially acceptable than the other. The pastoral counselor should recognize that any one may become addicted to a variety of substances. Being an addict or a potential addiction to anything, whether to alcohol, barbiturates, candy, tobacco, or some other substance, is not sinful or something for which anyone should be ashamed.

The first task of the pastoral counselor, when dealing with anyone who is addictively dependent, is to assure the client that there is absolutely nothing wrong, sinful, unnatural, or abnormal about addiction. Above all, the counselor should assure the individual that he or she has no reason to lose self-esteem, self-respect, and self-confidence; addiction is potentially possible for all fallible human beings and occurs in many lives. To help the client free himself or herself from the irrational guilt felt for addiction is the special and specific task of the pastoral counselor. Again, the counselor can only achieve this goal if he assists the client in distinguishing between himself as a noble but fallible human being and behavior that may not be approved by either the counselor or client when he is under the influence of the addictive substances.

2. The number and kinds of drugs being produced is increasing daily. Mention, therefore, of only a few and a minimal class of drugs is possible.

Drugs are classified into two categories; habit-forming and addictive drugs. The difference between these two depends on the physiological reaction to withdrawal from the drug. When one gives up a habit-forming drug, it may be missed because of the habit, but there are no physiological reactions. Withdrawal from addictive drugs is strikingly different; physical and physiological symptoms and problems, such as vomiting, headaches, nervous tremors, psychological anxiety, and fear, occur.

Two classes of habituating drugs are recognized: (1) *stimulants,* such as cocaine, and the amphetamines, such as Methedrine® and Benzedrine®; and (2) the *hallucinogens* from the mild hallucinogen, marijuana, to mescaline, psilocybin, and the more potent LSD.

Similarly, two classes of addictive drugs are recognized: (1) the *sedatives,* such as the barbiturates and other tranquilizers, the bromides, and alcohol; and (2) the *narcotics,* including the opium derivatives, particularly heroin, but also morphine, codeine, synthetic opiates, paregoric, and Demerol.

3. All drugs, including alcohol, affect the neurons, the cells of the nervous system. The stimulants cause the neurons to fire more rapidly; the tranquilizers slow down the firing of the neurons. The stimulants are habit-forming drugs and the tranquilizers addictive. One of the most frightening aspects of the misuse of drugs is the effects all have on the nervous system. There is a fundamental and inviolable law of nature that every created thing and being seeks homeostasis or equilibrium. When one tampers with the neurons of the nervous system and their firing, homeostasis is disturbed. If a drug speeds up the action of the neurons, there must be a reaction in the opposite direction when the drug is withdrawn; the converse is also true. For example, when the drug alcohol is used, it is a central nervous system depressant. However, when one withdraws from alcohol, there is often a reaction in the opposite direction,

including the speeding up of neuron firing. This may account
for some of the withdrawal symptoms, commonly called D.T.'s.

4. The counselor should avoid extremes in dealing with the
subject of drugs and addiction: He should help a client understand the dangers of misuses of any and all drugs; conversely,
an attitude that all drugs should be banned because they are
subject to misuse is unrealistic. A prudish attitude toward
drugs and addiction, including alcohol addiction, drives many,
especially young people who need counseling, away. The counselor's attitude should be that it is not the use but the abuse of
any created substance, including alcohol and other drugs, that
is wrong. Even the drug alcohol can have its positive uses: It
can be used medicinally. Used in moderation, it can be a source
of personal euphoria and a social catalyst. On the other hand,
when it is used excessively by an individual to escape anxiety,
frustrations, and stresses and strains, the possibility of addiction should be considered. When an individual loses his or her
freedom to control the drinking, alcohol addiction is a definite
probability.

5. Many drug-dependent individuals and those with alcohol
problems have been shown to be persons with poor self-
concepts and who feel inadequate. Addictive drinking has been
found to be a cause for further undermining of the self-concept
and causing the individual to feel increasingly inadequate.
This is tragic enough. However, there appears to be a more
serious potential consequence from drug addiction, such as
dependency on heroin and other hard drugs. Many times, particularly in the young, there seems to be a complete personality
change. Many become antisocial and sociopathic in their behavior. Many turn to crime to obtain the funds to sustain the
drug habit. With these, it is often necessary, at least at the
outset, for a counselor to take a firm stand and throughout the
counseling to point out and discuss with the individual the
potential personal and social consequences of the deviant behavior and continued use of a drug. In many cases, consideration of possible serious consequences of continued drug use
and atypical behavior is the only approach that can serve to
motivate, particularly, young offenders and drug-dependent

individuals. The counselor should remember, however, that there are no hopeless cases. It may take time and patience, but fortunately in many cases, the pain becomes great enough for the individual before it is too late to seek counseling.

CHAPTER 9

CASE STUDIES OF ATYPICAL ACTING OUT AND ANTISOCIAL BEHAVIOR

Billy

Case Presentation

As A PASTOR of a small parish in a remote area of the South, I had to assume many roles, from preaching on Sunday morning to assisting Dr. Watkins deliver a baby later in the day. I was not surprised, then, when our only policeman brought Billy Hanley to my office. He was accompanied by his mother, who had obviously been crying.

Officer Taylor explained that this was the third time he had caught Billy stealing things from the variety store. Twice he had taken him home with a warning, but now he did not know what to do but to put him in jail and wait to see what Judge Saunders wanted to do when he came the following week. He might send Billy to a reform school, make his family pay a heavy fine, or both. The officer did not know what the judge would do. I prevailed on Officer Taylor to let me talk with Billy and try to help him. If he stole again, I promised I would not try to stop having Billy placed in jail, but I would like one chance to see what I could do. The officer agreed.

I had known Billy all his life. He was now twelve years of age. He and his mother had lived alone after his father died when Billy was five years old. His mother was devoted to him. Except for the long hours she spent in her tiny florist shop and garden, Billy was her whole world. Approximately three years ago, however, his mother had met a man at a garden show. He was from Holland and spoke very little English. Because of their mutual interest in flowers, they began to see a

114

good deal of each other. Two years later they were married. Billy's mother was happy. As she said "Not only have I a fine husband who shares my love of flowers and plants, but it will give Billy a father. My new husband and I plan to expand my business so that we will have a large garden where we can grow vegetables as well as our flowers." Then it appeared everything would work out; apparently something went wrong.

Procedures

Billy was somewhat shy, a towheaded, thin young man with light blue eyes. At school, he usually stayed by himself and had no close friends. Knowing that I should not approach Billy as if to reprimand or punish, as he was in pain and needed help, I decided a paternal supportive approach would be most effective. However, it would be made clear that his behavior would not be condoned. Approval would not help Billy. It would be necessary for me to make it clear to Billy that I could and did love him as a father but, at the same time, did not approve of his behavior.

Counseling and Discussion

Our first session seemed futile. Billy just sat, and all he said was, "I don't know why I do it. I don't need the things I steal. I have my allowance and can buy what I want. I don't know why I get a kick out of taking things; lots of them aren't worth anything and I don't really want them. Most of the time, after my mother finds out and scolds me, I take them back and the store man doesn't even know I've taken them. I just don't know why I like to take things. I know it's wrong, but I still like to."

This was the extent of our first counseling session, and Billy promised to return the next day. In the meantime, I got out the psychology texts I had studied in college and seminary. Since there was no trained clinician in the town to whom I could turn, I would have to use my own resources.

After I spent several hours studying, it was clear that Billy's atypical acting-out behavior was a kind of *kleptomania* defined as "an irresistible compulsion to steal, usually without any use for the article stolen." This fit Billy's behavior exactly. The question in my mind was why? I could not explain his irrational behavior. I would need to consult a clinical psychologist when I went to the city towards the end of the week. When Billy came the next day, he contributed little to my understanding of his actions. We had, however, established a relationship that made it comfortable for Billy to talk.

When I saw Dr. Kinsolving, I told him about Billy. Billy knew I was going to do so and said I could. After hearing about Billy and his family situation, the doctor made two important observations: (1) Kleptomania is often an attempt to get attention when one feels unloved. In a sense, it is a symbolic act. The person takes things that do not belong to him to symbolize the need for a love he feels he has lost. (2) Often, lonely children who have been pampered and indulged find, often without any conscious awareness, that if he or she cannot get the attention of a loved one by being good, it can be obtained by being naughty. Without realizing it, when the parent pays attention to the child in such a situation, he or she is rewarding negative behavior and reinforcing the child's conviction that, to continue to receive parental attention, one must act in a negative manner.

As I drove home, some pieces, as in a jigsaw puzzle, began to fit together. After Billy's father died, his mother had smothered him with maternal affection. Later, in one of our conversations, Billy confirmed the fact that when he wanted his mother's attention all he had to do, as a small child, was scream and act like he was going to choke to death. She always came to him and made over him. Then there was a significant event. Billy's mother married again. Now she had another love object. Billy could not command all of her attention. As he indicated in one of our sessions, it seemed she never had any time for Billy. When this feeling came to Billy, his stealing began. Thus, by stealing, Billy not only symbolized his need for something to replace the lost love he felt but also caused his mother to pay attention to him.

I could not hope to deal with these underlying problems for Billy's behavior, but Dr. Kinsolving had suggested that I talk to his mother and stepfather with two purposes in mind: (1) to help them find ways to make Billy feel wanted and loved by both of them, and (2) to avoid, at all costs, rewarding negative behavior on his part. The best attitude when he acted out in a negative manner was not to scold or criticize, but ignore him: This would be more painful for one begging for love than any punishment.

With his stepfather, I explored possible ways in which the two might become better friends and companions. The solution was amazingly simple. We found Billy loved flowers and gardening as much as his mother and stepfather. They had never even considered it. His stepfather Henry, resolved to have Billy help him in the garden and decided to let Billy have a parcel of ground where he could have his own special garden. In time, this newfound relationship, particularly with his stepfather, was therapeutic for Billy. He never stole again.

I still had much to do where Billy was concerned. He was a pious and sensitive young man. It was difficult to help Billy get over his feelings of guilt for stealing, although the guilt was irrational, since it resulted from irrational behavior.

Our biggest task was to help Billy grow up and develop a mature adult value system. It was necessary to convince Billy that negative behavior might get attention from loved ones but would only lead to trouble for the one acting out. Ultimately, it would cost him the love of the one from whom he was trying to get attention. Billy and I worked for at least a year, once a week. For the next few years, he came back once or twice a month. His value system began to expand to include not only religious and spiritual values but also goals and material values for the future.

Evaluation and Results

When Billy was twenty-two, he went to California to live with an uncle. I did not hear from him for some time. However, I learned from his mother that he had married and now was starting his own business. He was buying a plot of ground and was going to grow and sell oranges.

Denise

Case Presentation

As the mother superior of a convent, one is naturally concerned about the sisters and those who want to become sisters,
the novices. Ours was a community who had a home for the
aged. Occasionally, we taught catechism in one of the local
churches. It was through our catechetical work that Denise met
us and decided she wanted to become a part of the community.

Denise was an only child. Her father died when she was nine.
her mother remarried a well-to-do merchant. All admitted that
he spoiled "his two girls," as he liked to call his wife and
stepdaughter. I was surprised, then, when Denise decided to
seek admission to the convent. Her mother and stepfather intended to sell their home and move to the Midwest. Denise did
not want to go. I wondered if this had not influenced her decision.

When Denise asked for admission to the convent, there were
several on the executive staff who wondered about her and if
she really had a vocation. It was only fair, however, to give her
a chance to test her potential vocation. It would then be for the
community to decide if she really belonged in the cloister.

Denise became a postulant when she was nineteen. This is
the step before the novitiate. During the next two years, I
watched her closely. They were hard years both for her and for
the community. She was very immature and spoiled. In spite of
all admonitions to be humble and unselfish, Denise would
pout if she did not get her way. The novice mistress came often
to my office and expressed her doubts about the suitability of
Denise as a candidate for the life of a religious.

To me Denise had become somewhat annoying and a nuisance. Daily she would run to me for attention that would have
been more appropriate for a mother to give to a five-or six-year-
old child. I had never seen a young woman of her age who was
so dependent. I guessed it was due to her doting mother and
stepfather, who pampered her and indulged her every whim

and desire.

Often, we questioned if she should remain. We did not have to decide. One day she came to my office to announce that she was leaving. I asked her why. She replied, "Well, Mother, you know they assigned us new rooms this week. I told Sister Helena (the novice mistress) that I wanted the end room because it had an extra window in it. I expected to get it. Instead, she gave it to that horrible Julia Ann. I'm simply not going to be treated this way. Everyone picks on me. I'm leaving." I said nothing; it was her decision.

I did not see Denise again for nearly a year and a half. I was surprised one evening when I received a message that a former novice was here and would like to see me. I said I would be happy to do so.

Denise, looking much older than when she had left the convent, came into my office. After we greeted each other, she began, "When I left the convent, I went to the city. I saw an ad in a newspaper that a wealthy widow would like a young lady as traveling companion for a trip to Europe with a lengthy stay on the Riviera. I applied for the position and got it." She paused for a moment. "Mrs. Snyder seemed the answer to my dreams. I would not have to work hard. She told me she would buy me pretty dresses and take me to the most elegant restaurants, the theater, and the races, and I would meet the finest people. It sounded wonderful. the only reason she required my services she said was that she did not like to travel alone." She paused. "This was not true. We had no more than arrived in Europe than she began to give me orders — do this — do that. I tried, but nothing seemed to please her. For example, after doing my best to iron one of her evening gowns, all she could say was, 'It looks awful. Do it again.' I never seemed to please her. What a selfish, self-centered person. No wonder she was lonely. She cared about no one but herself." Denise paused and blushed, "Yes, I know Mother, I saw in her a lot of me." Denise looked at me and then continued. "I was stuck; I had to accompany her until we could get back to the States. I became practically a slave. It was painful, but I think I've learned a lot." She paused for a long time. "Mother, I feel God works in strange ways. I know what an impossible spoiled brat I was when I was here, but, I know I can change with God's help and yours and the community. Mother, do you think I could have another chance?" I nodded approval.

Procedures

Since I was to be her personal counselor and spiritual director, I determined that the best approach to counseling Denise would be to discourage immature dependency. For this reason, the sessions were structured. She was to come at a given time. The sessions would be of a definite determined duration, and there would be homework after each session.

Counseling and Discussion

At the beginning, the homework consisted of Denise recording those incidents and occurrences in the past that seemed pleasant to her and those that seemed unpleasant. She was then instructed to set down what she considered to be strengths and weaknesses, talents, and shortcomings. From a consideration of all these, it became clear to Denise that when she had acted selfishly and with no consideration of others it had resulted in unhappiness for all concerned. However, when she had done something for someone else, it led to a lasting type of pleasure and happiness; she had been rewarded doubly. She finally concluded that when she had made another person happy she had found peace and satisfaction in herself.

We then began to set goals for the future. As the counseling continued, it became increasingly clear to Denise that her own happiness and fulfillment came in a large measure from helping others find peace and contentment. When she had reached this point in our counseling, all felt that she belonged in the community serving the needs of the aged and unwanted.

Evaluation and Results

Denise found the life she wanted in the convent, serving both the other sisters and the elderly men and women. As she grew older, Our Lord's words had more meaning: "He that loseth his life for My sake shall find it." (Matt. 11:39)

Anthony

I met Anthony for the first time when he was brought to me by his friend, Leonard, who was also a friend of Priscilla. Priscilla was pregnant; Anthony was responsible. Leonard brought him to me to discuss the possibility of marriage. I asked Anthony to first tell me something about himself. His exact words follow.

"My parents, a few years after marriage, got into frequent arguments. My father would knock my mother and me around. I left the house when I was sixteen, and my brothers and sisters also left at an early age, before twenty. Only one sister remained home. She's almost twenty. I often wrestled my father down to keep him from hitting my mother. I didn't date much as a boy. At sixteen, I went into the Marines. No serious romances before Priscilla, although I had at least a dozen affairs. I had no goals when I met Priscilla, and still don't. My old man raised me hard, and I was a hard case. I was emotionally defensive — couldn't express the emotions I felt well at all. I pent them up and when they did come out, they blew the walls down."

I had read about emotionally unstable personalities. They were described as excitable and ineffective in the face of minor stresses. They fluctuated in emotional attitudes that could upset interpersonal relations and impair judgment. Poorly controlled hostility, guilt, and anxiety were also present. This seemed to fit the acting-out behavior of Anthony.

The question then of marriage came up. Anthony immediately declared "Priscilla is a great gal and would make another man a fine wife, but not me. I'm immature and simply not able to enter into a lifelong thing like marriage. I just couldn't."

This seemed to end the matter, and I urged Leonard to talk to Priscilla and discourage any idea she might have for marriage. We could arrange to handle the pregnancy, but marriage was not the answer.

I thought I had seen the last of Anthony. It was not true. Three years after I first met him, a stranger knocked on my door. I did not recognize him. It was Anthony. He had a scar on his left cheek and he looked ten years older than when I last had seen him.

He began "I guess you're wondering what I'm doing here. Well, it's not too easy to explain. Maybe, I'd better begin at the beginning. You probably don't remember that I told you about my family, how my dad and mother fought and all us kids left home except one, her name's Susan. Well, you probably read in the papers, Mother and Dad were killed in a car accident about a year ago. We sold the house, and with the money I got, I rented a place for Susan and me to live and opened my own car body shop.

"I was doing real well, I thought; had a lot of girls — one-night stands, you understand — nothing serious. Susan got a job with one of the trucking companies; she was a secretary for one of the big shots. Anyway, I thought everything was going well until Susan came to my room one night and told me she had to talk with someone. I said okay; this wasn't like us to have a chummy brother and sister relationship — she did her thing and I did mine. However, she was my sister, and I felt kind a responsible for her. 'Well,' she began, 'I might as well tell you I'm pregnant.' I wasn't quite ready for that — she didn't date; she seemed like a real wallflower to me. So, I asked her who did it. She waited a while, and then said, 'My boss.' "

Anthony stopped for breath and then continued. "I couldn't believe it! He's an old man and has a wife and kids. What was he doing fooling around with my sister? I decided I was going to find out." Again, he paused. "I sure found out — I went to his office and told him what my sister had said. He laughed and said, 'What do you think you tramps are for anyway?' Boy, that made me mad, and I started to hit him when he picked up a sharp letter opener he had on his desk and let me have it across the cheek. I began bleeding, but he continued to laugh. I knew I was licked and hurt, so I left and went to the hospital's emergency room. I told them I fell on a piece of broken glass.

They had to take four stitches, and I still have a scar. You can see it, can't you?" I nodded that I could.

"Well anyway," he continued, "I sent Susan to my Aunt Martha's and they took care of the kid. I don't know exactly what happened, but I think they gave it away for adoption. Susan is still at Aunt Martha's. She doesn't want to come back here, so she got a job where Martha lives."

There was a long pause, and then Anthony said, "You know, I got to thinking after all this happened and what Susan's boss said, and I began to realize that I have treated at least ten or fifteen gals the same way Susan was treated by her boss. I know how mad I got. What happened to her didn't seem right. Then I got to thinking. I have been as big a jerk — or bigger — than he was. It's not right. I've got to change my outlook. That's why I have come to you. I've got to straighten up and fly right, or it's bad news."

He didn't need to say anymore. We had a great deal to do. In his own way, he had to find forgiveness for the guilt he felt for his actions. More important, together we needed to examine his theology and his value system so that goals could be set for the future that could be rewarding, sustaining, and energizing for him. He already had a trade. He loved to work with automobiles and was an expert mechanic. He lacked most of all meaningful and deep relationships with other people. This would take time. However, it was not impossible. He could develop those interpersonal relationships which he needed and wanted if he practiced the Golden Rule: "Whatsoever you would that men should do to you, do you even so to them." (Matt. 7:12)

CHAPTER 10

CASE STUDIES OF ALCOHOL DEPENDENCY, SOCIOPATHOLOGY, AND DRUG ADDICTION

Father Pat

COUNSELING another priest is often a hard task for even the most experienced pastoral counselor. It is often difficult for the potential client to dissociate himself from the relation of priest to priest and accept the counselor-client relationship. For this reason, I rarely take priests as clients. However, in the case of Father Pat, I could not say no.

One evening I was called by a close friend of mine, Father Mark. He asked me to do what I could for his friend, Father Pat. I was told that Pat had a serious drinking problem. Everyone had noticed it but had tried to cover it and said nothing to him about it. Now, he was in serious trouble. He was arrested for reckless driving at a high speed while intoxicated. It was possible he would have to go to jail. In court, however, a compromise was reached. He must take a special course in safe driving and go to a qualified alcoholics' counselor for help. He knew of me and asked that I be contacted, since there were many things about his personal life, including his sexual preferences, that he did not care to have exposed to any other counselor.

I said I would do what I could and made an appointment for the following evening. Father Pat arrived. He was about thirty-five years of age, a handsome, well-built Irishman. After a few preliminaries, we began to discuss his problem with alcohol.

I was unhappy to hear him say, "Well, Father, I can handle it. It's just that I wasn't feeling too good that night and the martinis went to my head. It won't happen again. I'm glad I could come to you, for I know you will understand."

To myself, I said, "Yes, I understand only too well. Pat, you want to quit hurting and get out of your present situation, but you have no intention to quit drinking." I was convinced he was not interested in counseling but was using his coming to see me as a cover-up to avoid any change and to satisfy the court.

The next few appointments proved that I was correct. First, he called to cancel an appointment because "something had come up." When he returned he said, "I've been so busy, I didn't have a chance to do the homework you gave me. I'll try to get it done before next time."

In the most pleasant way I could, I told Pat I felt he was a real phony, kidding himself and trying to kid me, and I suggested he stop it. He finally admitted, "I've always been a phony. You're right, I really only wanted to use you to get out of going to jail." He seemed relieved that I understood. "However," he continued, "I do want you to stick by me." I said I would be happy to do what I could, but little could be done until he was willing to face his problem with alcohol and do something about it. Only then could we establish a counseling relationship to deal with his personal problem. He assured me he would cooperate. That is the last I saw of him for six weeks, although he was supposed to have an appointment every Monday night. Moreover, he no longer bothered to call and cancel. This, I thought, might terminate our relationship.

One evening I got a call from Father Mark. Pat had been picked up in a neighboring city on another charge of drunken driving. Soon thereafter, I received a call from Pat to assure me that he wasn't drunk. "I only had one martini. I wasn't drunk. I don't know why I was picked up." He evaded the charge by paying a fine and telling them that he was under my "pastoral and clinical care." Unfortunately, he convinced the arresting officer and the court that this was true.

I did not hear from Pat for several weeks. Then, he called in panic. He had been arrested for knocking down a pedestrian when he was driving under the influence of liquor. He called to say he was leaving the state for the Midwest. He had hired a lawyer and was going to an alcohol treatment center for priests where he would remain until he returned for trial. His final words were, "I should have listened rather than being so smart. Now I know I have an alcoholic problem. You know, I don't even remember getting into my car and would not have known I hit that woman if I had not been told so after I sobered up in jail." Then he added, "Will you help me when I come back? I need it." I agreed, for I felt he had taken the first step toward health; he admitted he had a problem with alcohol and was willing to do something about it.

It was almost three months before I saw Pat again. He returned for trial. Happily, the woman lived and refused to press charges. He was given a suspended sentence and placed on probation for two years. He would not have a problem with driving for some time, as his driver's license was revoked indefinitely.

In the weeks that followed, I was able to establish a new relationship with a changed Pat. He knew that he could not drink and was using Alcoholics Anonymous as his means to stay sober "one day at a time." When I saw him he had not had a drink since the nearly fatal accident.

It had taken a long time, but anyone who counsels a person with an alcohol problem must understand that until a person accepts the fact that he has a problem, knows there is no cure, and is willing to try to abstain altogether from alcohol, nothing can be done to counsel him about any other problem, including the problems that may have led to excessive drinking in the first place.

Pat knew as we began our new counseling relationship that excuses for not doing his part in the process would not be tolerated. He could take it or leave it, but there would be no nonsense. He accepted my conditions for counseling.

In the weeks that followed, it became increasingly clear that Pat, in spite of his bravado and good looks, felt basically inadequate and had poor self-esteem and self-confidence. Pat discussed his early life. He had come from a humble, poor family. His father was a laborer in a construction company. Pat was not sure he should have enterd the seminary, but it meant so much to his parents to have a "priest-son," he reluctantly agreed to go. He liked it well enough, he stated, but he was not a good student and always felt inferior to most of the other students. Nonetheless, he was ordained and did well in his first assignments as an assistant. His trouble began when he was given a parish of his own. He was convinced he could not handle the responsibility. This is when his heavy drinking began.

Soon he asked the bishop to relieve him of his pastoral responsibilities. The bishop could not understand why but acceded to his wishes. Unfortunately, he made him a pastor of another parish, this time a pastor in an isolated community far removed from the city and most of his fellow priests. Excessive daily drinking began. As he said, "At first, I used the bottle to control myself, but soon it became the bottle that controlled me — night and day. I should have accepted the fact that I had a problem, but I was kidding myself.

My work became so poor that I was sent back to be an assistant in a large parish. I seemed to do well until the pastor went on vacation and I had to take over the responsibility of the parish. Everytime he went away I got drunk, and blew it."

"And," I added, "each time you did this your feeling of self-esteem and self worth went down and down; isn't that true?" He nodded in assent. It was clear that in spite of all his seminary training, he had not learned that he was important and worth something to himself and to his fellow men. My task was to help Pat develop a new value system that would lead to self-confidence, self-acceptance, and self-respect. His theological training made it easier than in many cases. He had been taught that God made everyone uniquely in His own image and that he was not only a creature of God, but, through baptism, was a child of God and a heir of Heaven. To think any less was not only to insult his own person but also to question God's creation.

Based upon his theology, Pat and I worked to help him gain the self-assurance that would make it unnecessary for him to find escape mechanisms to avoid anxiety and responsibility. In time, he saw that alcohol had been precisely that mechanism. Unfortunately, he had become addicted. He could not use alcohol again. Further, he needed no crutches or mechanism to escape life and its stresses and strains. Instead, with God's help, he could learn to handle whatever pressure or anxiety might come to him. He learned to say with the Psalmist, "Yea, though I walk through the valley of the shadow of death, I will fear no evil: for thou art with me; thy rod and thy staff they comfort me. (Ps. 23:4)

Joyce

Joyce was the wife of an Air Force colonel living in my parish. I had heard rumors that Joyce had an alcohol problem. I had not had any personal contact with her until her mother, Mrs. Riley, brought her to my office. She had been called by Joyce's husband, Kenneth. He informed her that he had had enough. He was going to divorce Joyce and move elsewhere. He would take their three small children with him. Mrs. Riley asked him to wait until she could come and talk to her daughter, and he agreed.

When Mrs. Riley arrived, she was dumbfounded. The house was filthy and liquor bottles were everywhere. The children were crying. Unwashed baby diapers, rotting food, and urine created a stench that was almost unbearable. When Mrs. Riley arrived, Joyce was drunk. She had passed out and was now slumped limply in a chair. A half-burned cigarette was still held in her hand. It could have burned her; she would not have known it. When she was aroused all she could say with a silly grin on her face was, "Hi, Mam. What's new?" She lapsed back into her drunken coma.

Mrs. Riley did what she could for the children and the house. When Kenneth came home, they did not need to say anything. Mrs. Riley begged for time to do something about Joyce's condition. Kenneth agreed, on the condition that Mrs. Riley would remain and take care of Joyce and the children.

It was decided to bring Joyce to me since I had some experience in counseling individuals with alcohol problems. Joyce accompanied her mother to my office the following day. It was evident that she did not want to be there and resented any interference in her life. "Sure," she said, "I know I've got a problem with alcohol, but who doesn't have a problem? Drinking makes me feel good . . . if I've got to have something wrong, I'm glad its booze." It was clear she had no intention of giving up alcohol at this point. Her mother and I tried to explain that Kenneth would leave her and take the children if she did not stop drinking. "Oh nuts," she replied, "he won't do that. He just says it to scare all of you and to make me stop drinking. He never will do it; he's too big a coward." It turned out this was not true. Three days later a note was found by Mrs. Riley that the colonel had asked for a transfer and received it. He had moved and taken the children with him.

Later that evening, I received a telephone call from Joyce. Obviously, she had been drinking. She began with slurred speech while crying intermittently telling me that Kenneth had gone. She kept saying, "What shall I do?" After many years of experience, I had learned *one can never reason with someone when he or she is drunk.* There is no use trying. The person is irrational, and some believe psychotic, when drunk. Sometimes, such an individual may fool another person and seem rational, but it is not true.

My answer to her was, "The only thing you can do is sober up. Until you do, don't bother me."

She continued, "But if you don't help me right now I will kill myself."

I again repeated, "I can't help you when you're drunk. There is no use continuing this conversation. I hope you will do nothing to yourself, but there is nothing I can do at this point." I hung up and said a silent prayer that she would not do something desperate or that would endanger her life.

I did not see Joyce for several days. When she came to my office, I noticed a change. She was no longer arrogant or hostile. In addition, she was sober. I invited her into my office. She sat for awhile and then began, "I really didn't think he would do it. What shall I do? I want him and the children." She began to cry.

After she had composed herself, I said, "the first thing you can do is to admit that you have a problem with alcohol.

Through no fault of your own you are addicted to alcohol. This means you cannot use alcohol. For some reason, unknown to all of us at this time, some people lose their freedom to drink socially and adaptively. As AA says for such a person, 'One drink is too many and a thousand are not enough.'" I assured her there was no cause to feel ashamed. There are many addictions that afflict different people. However, for the one dependent on alcohol, there is no cure. It can be controlled but not cured.

It was hard for Joyce to accept what I had said to her. "It's a question of relative values, Joyce." I continued, "You can have the bottle and eventually a miserable death, or you can have your husband and children, but you can't have both." She sat for a while and then said, "I see what you mean — but — it isn't going to be easy." I suggested she go to AA for strength and support in her battle to abstain from alcohol. She agreed, provided I would contact her husband and say that she was going to try to become the wife he wanted and to completely control her drinking.

I contacted Kenneth, and he seemed happy. He informed me that soon he would be going overseas. He would see Joyce before he left and return the children to their home.

Joyce was finally motivated to change. Her husband and children meant more to her than anything in the world, even the bottle. She began to fight the long daily battle for sobriety and a new life.

Some months after Joyce had joined AA, I visited her home. It was spotless and the children clean and happy. On this visit, she informed me that she had visited a clinician about her nervous condition. He suggested that anxiety and tension had led her to the use of alcohol as a tranquilizer and sedative in the first place. Unfortunately, she became addicted. Further, during therapy, he found that she had no self-confidence and felt worthless both to herself and to others. It would be my task as a pastoral counselor to help Joyce develop a feeling of personal and social value based on her religious convictions and help her develop a new value system by which to live. She soon became an ideal client, following the instructions given her and cooperating in every way she could.

Joyce continued to visit the clinician at regular intervals. She had requested that he and I work together in her case. This was an ideal relationship and in her best interest.

There was one surprise for me. Dr. Hanson called me one day to tell me what he thought was the basic reason for Joyce's feeling of inadequacy and worthlessness. It seemed such a minor incident but was traumatic for Joyce. He informed me that he had Joyce write thirty minutes each day about her past life. One day, she brought her notes to the therapy session. In them she related how much she loved her mother as a little girl but how mother often didn't seem to have much time for her. When she was about five a painfully significant event occurred.

Joyce had watched her mother bake biscuits. One day when Joyce felt a special need for attention from her mother, she decided, while her mother was downtown shopping, to surprise her by baking some biscuits for her. It wasn't as easy as she thought. By the time she had finished there was flour, salt and pepper and pots and pans all over the kitchen. Unfortunately, also, the biscuits burned so that when her mother arrived home a dense cloud of black smoke was exuding from the oven. Not understanding the little girl's intention, Mrs. Riley shouted, "Joyce, you're no good; you never will be any good; you'll never amount to anything as a woman." This remained in Joyce's mind. Joyce assumed her mother was correct — she was no good and never would be any good. "After all, Mother is right about everything," she reasoned, "I never will amount to anything."

When such thoughts came to her mind in later life, Joyce took to the bottle to anesthetize herself and avoid the anxiety such thoughts brought to her. The statement seemed petty, but it was basic to her problem.

A time came when Mrs. Riley needed to know the truth. When she was told, she was stunned. She resolved to do what she could to remedy the situation. She was mature enough to go to Joyce, discuss the matter, apologize, and ask Joyce to forgive her. Although Joyce was now a grown woman and had children of her own, there was something still of the little girl in her, then with tears in her eyes, she threw her arms around her mother and received a big hug in return.

I have not seen Joyce for many years, but I understand she now lives with her husband at an Air Force base in Hawaii. I hear from the family each Christmas. They seem very happy.

Alfred Smithers

One of the most disagreeable men I had ever met was Alfred Smithers. He never had a kind word for anyone. He was harsh with all who worked under his supervision. At no time did he show any appreciation for the efforts of his secretaries and other staff. On the contrary, he was quick to find fault with them and criticize them for being a few minutes late. He never recommended any for a raise. In fact, he complained that there was no wonder he could get so little done with such an incompetent staff. One of his office help said that in eight years she had never seen him smile. One thing was sure; Alfred cared only about Alfred and no one else.

I discussed him with a friend of mine, a clinician. He had known Alfred for many years and was convinced he had an antisocial or sociopathic personality. "Such individuals," he said, "are characterized by unsatisfactory interpersonal relationships and are insensitive to the needs and feelings of others, in fact, to the ethical values of society in general.

Such individuals are often callous and interested only in themselves. Tragically, they are often intelligent. Many are professional people. But, they are completely self-centered; they never seem to learn from experience and couldn't care less about anyone else." I asked him what could be done for such a person. "Unfortunately, little or nothing. It takes a major personal calamity or tragedy to penetrate their rigid personal world. I don't like to take someone who is antisocial as a patient. If he is forced to come to me by someone else, I refuse to take the case. Only when he has hurt enough, personally, is he possibly amenable to treatment. My advice to you is to help those who work for him. Let them know that he is a sick man living in his own unhealthy personal world. Urge them to ignore him and what he says or does to them. It isn't easy to work under such conditions, but unless a person becomes objective and refuses to let it affect him emotionally, he can break under such stress and strain."

I went home. I counseled Cynthia, Alfred's personal secretary, along the lines my friend had recommended. In subsequent weeks, I worked with Cynthia using rational behavior techniques. We worked to help her eliminate the unwanted emotions, such as hostility, anger, and resentment, that she felt for her boss. This necessitated substituting rational thinking for the irrational thinking that had led to her unwanted emotions. For example, when Alfred had said, "You are the worst secretary I've ever known," Cynthia had felt hurt, angry, frustrated, and depressed. She had said to herself, "He has no right to treat me this way. He ought not to criticize and bark at me the way he does." We concluded after our RBT sessions that the rational thinking would be "Alfred is a sick man. I am sorry that he said what he did, but he said it, and he has a right to say what he wants. Further, I wish he liked me and my work. The fact is he doesn't and I can't change him. I can't really know, in fact, if he really feels that way. I can't get into his head and know what he really thinks." Cynthia substituted rational thinking. "I wish things were different, but Mr. Smithers is a sick man and I am not going to let him cause me to upset myself. After all, what I feel in my stomach depends on what I think in my head. It really doesn't depend on Mr. Smithers at all." After some practice, Cynthia was able to rationally control her emotions in regard to Mr. Smithers.

My next contact with anyone connected with Alfred was unpleasant. A woman, Dorothy, came to me. I learned that she and Alfred had slept together. She had become pregnant, and, on the spur of the moment, they had been married before a justice of the peace. She realized it was a mistake soon after the marriage. He seemed not to care about her at all. He wanted, it seemed a housekeeper, not a wife. At home, he was an "animal," especially when he was drunk and high on pot. His favorite pastime was to brag about his many sexual exploits. Within the first month, he stayed away from home seven nights. He taunted her with his claim that he had slept with seven different women on the nights he was not home. Dorothy was able to put up with his verbal abuse, but when he began beating and kicking her, she decided to leave. She returned to her parents' home and began divorce proceedings.

Alfred did not seem to care. He said to her, "It's good to get rid of you, and I sure don't want to be tied down to a kid. I only married you for convenience, but I got tired of you right off — I got to have more than one woman."

A break came for his office force. Alfred was offered a position in another firm, and he took the job. I, too, was glad he was leaving, although I hardly knew the man. I thought I would never see him again. This was not to be so.

Approximately two years after Alfred had taken his new position, a man came to my door. I did not recognize him. He had only one eye and he used a crutch because his left leg was useless. I invited him in, not knowing who he really was.

He began "You don't know who I am, do you?" I had to admit honestly that I did not. "Well, I'm Alfred Smithers." I was shocked. This did not look like the arrogant, self-assured man I had known a couple of years before. I said nothing. Alfred then continued, "I've come to you to get some help. It wasn't easy, but I know I need help and I didn't know anyone to come to but you." When he sensed I was willing to help if I could, he continued, "This isn't going to be easy, but if I don't get it off my chest you won't understand."

"You know a lot about me through Cynthia and others of my former office staff. You also knew Dorothy. She got a divorce. I don't know where she is now. Well, anyway, I took my new job and got myself a fancy apartment. I don't have to tell you but you know I have had a lot of women in my day — in fact, that's about all I enjoyed — not so much the sex as the conquest. Once I'd won a woman and had her for a night, I lost interest and would try to find another one. Everything seemed to be going well until about seven months ago. Then the roof fell in."

He paused for a few minutes, then continued. "One night a big, burly man weighing about 225 pounds and over six feet tall knocked on my door. When I went to the door, he said, 'Are you Alfred Smithers?' I answered that I was but what did I have to do with him. With that, he pushed his way into my apartment. He turned toward me angrily and said, 'Do you remember a pretty little blonde who worked at the delicatessen that you brought to your apartment a couple of months ago?' It was hard for me to remember — I had slept with so many. I answered, 'Did she have a large mole on the left side of her face?' 'That's her,' he said. 'Well, she's dead — and you killed her. She hadn't slept with nobody but you. She found out you gave her VD and she was probably pregnant. She cut her wrists and died before they could get her to the hospital.' Then it happened. He began beating on me and kicking me. I panicked and jumped through the window of my apartment. I lived on the second floor, so I thought I could make it. It wasn't true. Broken glass cut my eye, and when I hit the pavement, I'm told my leg was crushed by the impact of the fall. I don't know. I was unconscious. I woke up in the hospital. I learned my eye had to be removed and that I would never use my left leg again.

"I was in the hospital for four weeks. During that time I did a lot of thinking." He paused for a long time. Then with difficulty he continued, "I don't know what to do, but my way of living just isn't paying off. I know I need to change, but I don't know how. Maybe, you don't understand, but I never felt anything for anyone else and don't even know if I can. This is where you come in. I hope that you can help me to 'feel.' " I told him quite frankly I was not sure but would be willing to try.

This was the beginning. I learned as much from Alfred as he did from me. It seemed impossible that a human being existed who was unable to feel for others. Alfred was such a person. Literally, he had to learn to empathize. The only way he could learn was through teaching him to think what he wanted to feel. In a sense, we used rational behavior counseling in reverse. It was something new. Alfred had to think deliberately in a way so that he could produce what seemed to be appropriate feelings in response to other human beings.

Our counseling took many sessions. An altogether new value

system had to be developed for Alfred to include others and the world outside of himself. It was not easy for either of us, but I learned through Alfred that "there are no hopeless cases."

Amy and Tony

I found it difficult but a real challenge to try to counsel young men and women who lived in the halfway house for individuals addicted to drugs. Most of them were very young and in their early twenties. Many looked much older, as drugs had taken their toll.

I met Amy and Tony at the same time. They had been living together for five years, except for the time he spent in prison and she spent in a women's reformatory.

Their backgrounds were completely different. Amy had come from a middle-class, proper family in the Midwest. She was in her third year of high school when she got tired of the hum-drum life of her small community. She moved to the city and soon was lost in the ghetto and the commune in which she lived. Tony, on the other hand, knew nothing but the streets and life of the ghetto. He did not know who his father was and cared less about his mother, who was a prostitute. Amy and Tony met in the commune and then decided to go on their own and, as one put it, to "shack up together."

Both, in time, became addicted to heroin and were sentenced to prison and the reformatory for selling drugs on the street. Both had arrived at the same place in life when I met them. Counseling, however, would be different for both of them. Both were now hard and, to a degree, antisocial. They had arrived at similar attitudes toward themselves, others, and society from completely different backgrounds and points of view.

Amy felt inadequate and immature when she came to the city. Because of drugs and her life in the ghetto, her personality changed; she became hard, cold, and callous.

Tony's background was entirely different. He had known nothing but poverty, the streets, and "dog eat dog." He did not change in personality when he met Amy and they lived together. He had from early childhood developed a hard, cold, and self-defensive outlook on life. Counseling, then, would involve rehabilitation for Amy and habilitation for Tony. The goals in both cases would be the same; that is, to help Amy and Tony develop value systems and find goals that would assist them not only to kick their drug habits but also to give productive meaning to their lives.

I decided to see them separately, although I assured them I did not mind if they shared with each other what we had discussed in any counseling session.

I turned my attention first to Amy. She would be easier to counsel than Tony because of her background. Importantly, my approach to her did not suggest disapproval or censure. She had had enough of that from her family and others she knew. I accepted the fact that she lived as a common-law wife of Tony (although I did not approve) and that our main task was to develop new values so that Amy could find a new life. I could do nothing about her drug habit. This I left to those more competent. My task began when she had accepted the fact that she was an addict and that the addiction could not be cured and would have to be controlled through, at times, painful abstinence from drugs.

Our first session was productive. When she was sure that I was not going to chastise her or point out her mistakes and shortcomings, she began, "You know, I've learned an awful lot and I've done a lot of rotten things, but there's one thing that means a lot to me, that's Tony. I love that crazy guy. I want to build my life around him and what he wants. Do you think it can be done?" I assured her it could. We had a value to build on. Counseling would not be as difficult with Amy as I might have expected when I first met her.

When I first met Tony, I guessed that he was about twenty-seven years old, although he looked much older. I asked him if we could rap together. He agreed. I asked him about himself, and he responded.

"Oh, man, I've got a real thing. My old lady is a whore and I never met my father. I've been on the street all my life. You want to know about my habit don't you? Well, you know, it started when I was nine or ten, real easy like, a roach [marijuana or pot] maybe twice a day if I was lucky. [He then tried LSD and had some bad trips.] A couple of years later, I started using the soft stuff [barbiturates], but it didn't do nothing for me. Then I tried to turn on with speed [amphetamine], Coke [cocaine], and sniffin' poppers [amyl nitrite]. I got a few highs, but I didn't dig the arrangement. One day a dude offered me some of the real stuff. I sniffed it for a while, but then started shootin' horse [mainlining heroin]. I became a pusher. Made good money, but we needed a lot. Then Amy and I got caught. She went to a women's reformatory and I got prison, both of us for two years. We got out about six months ago and we got back on the stuff. Knew we needed help and that's why we're here. Getting methadone every day. Don't know if it's the answer but it keeps us from climbing the walls for the real stuff. We're both clean now — see my arms [needle marks disappeared]. One thing I don't dig — mixin' booze with pot and speed. I get all mixed up and fall out. Yea, and there's another thing, I don't, buy this new stuff — angel dust [pencyclidine (PCP), also known as "peace pills" and "killer weed"] — it makes you go out of your cool — a guy can blow a fuse. One of my buddies goes completely nuts; another one had to be put in a crazy house. No, man, that's not for me." He paused; it gave me a chance to translate what he had said.

For all his roughness and lack of polish, Tony was a warm and likeable person. He simply had not had a chance. I learned from the psychologist who tested the residents that Tony had a good mind but lacked the education he needed. It was suggested that he contact the educational therapist and work for his high school equivalency diploma.

When I suggested this to Tony, he looked sheepish and said, "Hey man, are you kiddin'? Me with a high school diploma. My gang won't believe it. Besides, what'll I do with it? It won't get bread [money] for me?"

I said to him, "You don't know; being able to read and write and having some education could help you get what you want."

All he said was, "okay, maybe you're right; I don't know."

It took a long time and a lot of rap sessions for Tony and I to help him develop a value system in place of the primitive survival of the fittest philosophy of the ghetto.

Together, we looked into his past. There was little to commend it. His life had been sordid, dirty, and unpleasant. New values had to be developed. To do this, it was necessary to look for latent talents or interests he might have. This took a great deal of time and effort. A goal for the future emerged slowly but importantly. Often Tony would say, "I'm sure gettin the breaks; I feel sorry for a bunch of those kids on my street that'll never have a chance and never make it. Those damn cops don't understand them and give 'em a break."

One day I said, casually, "Then, why don't you become a cop and help them?"

If I had hit him in the head with a brick, Tony could not have been more stunned: "What did you say, man? Me a cop! You must be out of your cool." I said no more but let Tony think about it. During the next sessions, I knew it was on his mind. Repeatedly he would say, "Me be a cop for the kids . . . that's the craziest idea I ever heard." Then, almost to himself, "Ah course, I'd sure understand them better than those flatfoots they got on our beat right now, but it's a crazy idea."

Along with fighting his drug problem, Tony began to wrestle with the idea of being a policeman trained to help youth and work in the ghetto. I said no more. It was up to Tony.

One day Tony came to my office. He brought Amy with him. He didn't know how to start but finally blurted out, "We've decided I'm going to police school and learn to help kids. I am scared to try it by myself, so I've asked Amy if she'd marry a no-good like me. She said she'd be willing to give it a try." I smiled at Amy because this was what she wanted most in life.

From there on counseling was with both Tony and Amy. Together, we developed a value system not only for their married life, but also for the vocation of each; Amy, the wife and helpmate for Tony, and for Tony, a family man working in the ghetto for his wife, and hopefully children, and for other "ghetto youth" who are less fortunate than the Tony and Amy I was privileged to counsel.

Part V
Other Persons in Pain

CHAPTER 11

CASE STUDIES INVOLVING
HUMAN SEXUALITY

THERE are many forces that may cause pain
for individuals. Some are cultural and others social, religious,
racial, or national. They result, however, in certain individuals'
behavior being considered by the society, by the individual, or
both as atypical and, in many instances, taboo and even pun-
ishable.

Nothing is the source of greater pain than social mores and
religious attitudes of many groups in the matter of human
sexuality. Even today, the modern Western world is infected
with the negative puritanical Protestant teachings and Catholic
Jansenistic repressive attitudes that preach or imply that sex is
something dirty and, to a certain degree, evil. As a reaction to
these repressive forces, the pendulum has swung in the opposite direction in many groups today, so that sexual license and
sex for its own sake has been even more popular and open. The
number of young men and women living in free-sex communes
and the partner-sexual-exchange parties, i.e. wife swapping, of
their elders has steadily increased. Many individuals are caught
between these extremes of repression and license and their actions judged by the subjective and often irrational attitude of
the society in which they live.

Of all the cases that come to a pastoral counselor because of
pain for atypical behavior, those involving violation or
seeming violation of sexual codes and prohibitions are most
numerous. This is particularly true where a repressive and
prudish attitude toward sex prevails. Unfortunately, the negative attitude of many religious denominations have occasioned
unnecessary pain and anguish for many whose sexual behavior
is considered evil and reprehensible. Many of these judgments
are subjective, irrational, and contrary to biological facts and to

143

the nature of man.

For effective pastoral counseling in the area of sexuality, at least six attitudes and approaches are essential.

1. Good counseling is not possible if the counselor holds a negative attitude toward sexuality. He must see it as something good and wholesome and sanctified by God Himself.

2. The counselor cannot be effective if he or she has a problem with his or her own sexuality and has not resolved it.

3. It is essential to get the facts. The counselor must know, for example, that science has shown that masturbation, in itself, need not affect a person physically or mentally. Ill effects result emotionally and psychologically only to those who are concerned that they have committed a forbidden or immoral act. Similarly, it is becoming more and more evident from scientific research that all humans are basically bisexual. There may be yet unknown genetic or possibly hormonal factors that predispose an individual toward homosexual or heterosexual behavior. However, it is known that environmental influences, early sex experiences, and opportunities, along with sex education, largely determine the direction of the sexual drive that is normal and natural for a given individual. Hence, homosexual and heterosexual attractions are both normal and potential for any and all human beings. Neither are unnatural or abnormal.

The matter of fetishes has been the cause of much controversy. A fetish is something animate or inanimate that is associated in the mind of a given individual with sexual pleasure. There is nothing wrong with fetishes as such. In fact, they can assist in sexual activity and pleasure in some cases. Is the fetish harmful or harmless? If it is not harmful for anyone concerned, there should be no problem. On the other hand, if it is dangerous or harmful for either party, it should be avoided.

4. Sex and sexual activity needs to be viewed in the context and perspective of the whole person. It is a person who performs a sexual act. Sex as an isolated entity is meaningless. The pastoral counselor must evaluate sexual activity in terms of the unique framework of an individual personality. There cannot be norms for sexual behavior, therefore, that can be applied rigidly and in exactly the same way to any two human beings.

Thus, the counselor needs not only to be positive in his attitude toward sex in general but also to be flexible enough to appraise sexual activity in terms of unique and whole persons with their own theologies and value systems. This leads to the next essential attitude and approach.

5. Regardless of his or her own theology and value system, the counselor must aid a client in formulating his or her own standards for sexual behavior and in determining a certain conscience regarding sexual activity.

As indicated earlier, as a Christian teacher, the counselor may try to influence an individual's theology and system of moral standards and values according to his or her own religious and moral convictions. This is valid if the pastoral counselor makes it known and the client accepts this role of counselor-teacher.

Assuming that the teacher has done all he can to persuade and convince the client of a given value system, the client must ultimately form his own. It is a principle of moral theology of many Christians that an individual is judged by God by what an individual, in his own subjective conscience, believes is true and not by what is objectively true if an individual has sincerely tried to know the truth.

6. Human sexuality is a wholesome, healthy gift of God. Regardless of what any man's theology or standards define as to the purpose or purposes of sexual activity, in most cases, sex finds its expression within deep interpersonal, shared, and endearing human relationships. It follows that to the degree sexual relationships are creative, energizing, and fulfilling for the individuals as human beings, to that degree they are positive and rewarding. Conversely, to the degree that they are destructive and involve violations of one's self or other human beings, to that degree they are negative and undesirable. A Christian may well ask him- or herself whether this sexual activity leads to greater self-fulfillment and self-actualization. Is it valuable, for the same reasons, for the one with whom he or she is engaging in sexual activity? Finally, is it leading away from God or closer to Him? These are the critical questions.

In the cases that follow, unlike earlier ones, the counselor is a pastor with some training in counseling and at least some knowledge of psychology and sexology.

Lowell

When I went to the door, Mrs. Harrison, one of the sacristans of the parish, asked if she could see me privately. I asked her to come in. As she sat down it was obvious she was very disturbed and also seemed embarrassed to start the conversation. Finally, she began, "It's — it's about Lowell." I was surprised, as I knew Lowell well. He was now twelve and one of my favorite altar boys. I knew that he lived alone with his mother, a widow. He was an excellent student, a bit shy and retiring and somewhat of a loner. All in all, however, he was an unusually fine person. I could not imagine what had come up regarding Lowell to cause Mrs. Harrison such distress.

She began again, "I really don't know how to say it — I'm so mixed up and ashamed."

I said "Now, Margaret, nothing could be as bad as all that — and you know we can discuss anything together."

She thought a moment. "I know we can discuss anything, but this is the most difficult matter I have ever had to discuss with you. I'm not by nature a nosy person. I respect Lowell's privacy and his right to have things all his own, something happened yesterday that was not planned. I was going to the bathroom. I did not know Lowell was there. For some reason, he had not locked the door. When I opened the door, I got the shock of my life — Lowell was masturbating. I didn't know what to do or say. He didn't either. I said nothing but ran to my room to compose myself. I did not know if I should have punished him immediately, ignored him, or what? I still don't know how to handle it. We ate supper together without looking at each other or saying anything. Now, what shall I do?"

"First, Margaret," I said, "you must realize that it is not unusual for a boy of his age to masturbate; in fact, it is quite common. In the second place, let me assure you that it will not harm his mind or body. Above all, I am glad that you did not punish him. That is the worst thing you could do, especially at the time he was probably reaching orgasm.

"I had the unhappy experience of counseling a young man in his early twenties. His father had caught him in the act of masturbation and angrily burned the boy's body in several places with his lighted cigarette. As a result of this experience, the young man adopted a masochistic attitude toward sex; that is, he needed to feel pain in order to be sexually aroused. Unfortunately, when he was twenty-four, he was killed by a sadistic individual who cut him with knives until he bled to death. Punishment is never the answer to one who is found masturbating; understanding is the important thing.

I think if I were you I would bring it up and let him know that his behavior does not in anyway change your feeling about him personally. Further, I would let him know that, naturally, you find it hard, as a woman, to understand the problems and concerns of a boy now growing into manhood. You may suggest to him that I would be willing to discuss not only the matter of masturbation with him, but also the many problems and interests that are natural for a teenage young man. You see, Margaret, what he did must be seen in the context of his whole personality and development. This is the age when both young men and young women seek to find a unique personal as well as a sexual identity. An act or acts of masturbation cannot be considered in isolation. They must be understood and dealt with in terms of the total individual who performs such acts." Margaret seemed relieved.

Two days later Lowell came to see me. When he felt certain that I was not going to chastise or ridicule him, we began talking of many things, including his goals and aspirations for the future.

Lowell needed an adult male figure in his life. I was privileged to be that man. I learned as much as Lowell did in the weekly sessions we had together.

Typically adolescent in his thinking and behavior, Lowell was struggling for independence but still needed to be dependent in many ways without being embarrassed or made to feel childish and immature. The challenge for any adult dealing with a teenager is to assist a young person to find his or her own personal identity but, at the same time, to permit the adolescent to feel free to rely and depend on the adult when he or she needs to do so.

On the other hand, the adult must avoid fostering an unhealthy dependency, which may be ego-satisfying to the adult but not in the best interest of the youth. Extremes can be avoided if the older person is guided by the needs of a youth. The adolescent is permitted to lean and depend on the adult only when he or she needs to do so and at no other time.

Educating and counseling Lowell in matters of sex involved at least three basic considerations. First, we discussed sex in its proper spiritual, religious, and personal context. My purpose was to assist Lowell to a positive and healthy attitude toward sex and to see sexual activity in the proper perspective of the human person as a whole. We studied the purposes for sexual activity and the possibility in the proper human context, not only of procreation, but also as a physical expression of a deep and meaningful interpersonal relationship.

Next, we studied together the anatomical and physical aspects of sex and sexual activity. Lowell learned to use the proper terms for the parts of the male and female body and for sexual activity. He soon became comfortable using the terms *penis* and *vagina* in our discussions, rather than the evasive terms that still reflect the influence of puritanism on our Western society.

As a pastoral counselor, it was essential that I guided Lowell in forming a certain conscience not only regarding masturbation but also other sexual acts. It was necessary initially to help Lowell understand that sexual urges, desires, and fantasies that arise spontaneously are determined by emotions and are not under the control of reason. They have no morality, no matter what they are, who the objects or individuals desired might be, or the intensity of the desires. These are animal emotions; they should not be causes for anxiety or concern. Learning this, Lowell's tension regarding sexual desires was noticeably alleviated, and he became more relaxed when he discussed his own sexual fantasies.

After this, it was necessary to help Lowell form a certain

conscience about sexual behavior. This took some time. I made it clear to him that I had a certain conscience based upon my religious and theological convictions. I could hope that he would form his conscience along the same lines. After much discussion, Lowell decided on what he thought was right and wrong in matters of sex, including masturbation. He then began to live according to his own moral standards and code.

In matters of sex and sexual activity, I served primarily as Lowell's teacher. As a counselor it was my role to assist him in developing his value system and to explore with him his talents, interests, aspirations, and realistic potential goals. We agreed that his value system should help him become a mature adult; his goals and aspirations should be energizing and creative. He recognized that in his adolescent years he had begun the search for personal integrity and identity and that his value system should include ways and means to arrive at a mature adult self-concept and identity. It should include not only those things that would lead Lowell to self-actualization but also provide for potential deep interpersonal relations. Above all, it must include theological and religious values, including those that would not only sustain him in the present life but also are important to his belief in a life after death.

It was too early in Lowell's life to determine the exact vocation he should follow. However, based upon his interests and talents, we considered the possibility of many alternatives. There would be plenty of time after he finished a college preparatory course in high school and a general arts and science course in college to make a decision.

Lowell liked art and music. Even if he would not become a professional, he was encouraged to use them as hobbies and avocations. Finally, the use of his leisure time and ways to communicate and relate with his peers were considered important subjects for us to discuss.

With pride, Margaret and I watched Lowell grow from an awkward, shy, pimple-faced adolescent to a self-assured young man. It was no surprise that he chose medicine as his profesion. In later years, he became a heart specialist.

Dorothy

Dorothy Spraggs was one of the loveliest women I had ever known. She and her husband had moved into my rural parish when she was about thirty-one years of age. Tom, her husband, commuted to the city each day where he had his law practice. When asked why they moved from the city, Dorothy said, "We thought it would be nice to live out here in the country where we could have a garden, fresh air, the lake, and the out-of-doors."

Dorothy came to me each week for spiritual direction. In addition, she assisted at weekday Masses as well as on Sunday. She worked in the sacristy and in the church school on Sunday mornings. At any time, she was willing to help around the church, even to cleaning the pews when the janitor was not there. Dorothy and Tom were childless, so that she had ample time. All they had was each other, but they seemed completely devoted to each other.

At all times, Dorothy appeared as a woman who was naturally tense and high-strung. No one would, however, suspect the pain and anguish Dorothy felt most of the time. As her counselor and confessor, I learned that she had developed a habit of masturbation, which she detested. At least once a week she would ask to go to confession and there ask for forgiveness and sob out her agony and frustration. Each time, she would resolve never to masturbate again, but the habit persisted.

Dorothy considered her actions seriously sinful. I assured her that habit lessened or eliminated guilt all together if one was doing all that he or she could to break the habit. This did not satisfy Dorothy.

All attempts at counseling were to no avail. I knew that such acts could only be understood in terms of the whole personality of an individual and could not be treated as isolated behavior. Because of this, I suggested she go to Dr. Lewis for a complete physical examination. With her consent, the doctor and I were free to discuss and consult each other regarding her.

After the examination, Dr. Lewis informed me that Dorothy

was suffering from hypertension and a digestive disorder. Undoubtedly, her high blood pressure and overactive digestive system contributed to her personality problem, but they were not the answer. Dr. Lewis gave her tranquilizers and other medications. These seemed to calm Dorothy, and masturbation became less frequent, but this was not the solution. I decided to establish a counselor-client relationship with her to see if, together, we would find some answers and means to help her.

We did not need to spend much time on the subject of guilt. She was convinced it was wrong to masturbate. In fact, she was overly concerned, almost to the point of scrupulosity. Repeatedly, I had to remind her that her habit lessened or eliminated moral guilt. She was not satisfied.

In our formal counseling, we took a look at Dorothy's past. Each time she came for counseling, she was required to bring a written report of her recollection over a given period of time in her life history. One of the reports conveyed significant information. She wrote "I am an only child but I had a lot of relatives who lived in the same apartment house where my mother and dad lived. I never had to be alone. I hate to be alone. Dad was a pharmacist; he's now retired. My mother and dad are devout Catholics. I was brought up to follow the faith according to the way I had been taught by my parents, the priests, and the sisters in the school. I was not sure what to do when my cousin in the same school masturbated in front of me and suggested I do the same thing. It didn't seem to bother her — as a sin — I mean, but it really bothered me, although I got a good feeling in my body when I did it. I didn't do it very often after that first time. I wouldn't say it began to be a habit until about the time we moved here three years ago. I don't know why doing it increased when we came here. If we can find out it might help me get over it." Again, I assured her that I knew she was trying. Above all, if she did have a "fall," as she called it, she was not to get discouraged but realize that it takes a long time to break any habit.

One thing became increasingly apparent. The habit had become compulsive behavior only after Dorothy and Tom had moved to the country. I decided we should investigate the reason. During one of the sessions, I said to Dorothy, "Why do you think it got worse when you moved here?"

She thought for a minute, then answered "I don't know, I really don't. All I can think of is I haven't anything to do when Tom is in the city — which is most of the time — except help here at the church once in a while. I really haven't anything to do most of my day. I get tired of reading and watching TV. I don't play bridge and don't have any friends to visit or go with to a show or something." She paused. "I simply have a lot of time on my hands and don't know what to do with it. I'm so bored and lonely most of the time. There's nothing worse than being bored unless it's being alone. I live for Tom to come home — nothing else." Again she paused, then added, "I know it's awful to say, but I wish we would go back to the city where we belong. I'm so lonely out here by myself. I feel like screaming half the time. Things haven't worked out the way Tom and I planned. We don't have a garden; Tom hasn't the time to make one, and I don't know how and don't want to learn. After he's commuted sixty-five miles to work and sixty-five back, Tom is too tired to do anything. After he gets home, he has his supper and goes to bed. Poor Tom, it's so hard on him. I never have told him how I hate it here. I'm afraid it would break his heart. He always dreamed of a little cottage in the country and near a lake." She thought for a moment, then continued, "Not having any children makes it even harder. We both want them so badly, but I can't have them.

Dorothy fell silent; however, I had a better understanding of her masturbatory problems in terms of her whole personality and life situation. Here was a painfully lonely young woman, childless, with nothing to do but wait all day for the return of a tired husband who could not give her the companionship she needed so badly. What a contrast this life was for Dorothy, compared to the warm interpersonal relationships and activities she enjoyed with her family and friends in the city. I asked her if she would be willing for me to discuss with them their living situation. Of course, there would be no mention or hint of her masturbatory problem. I simply wanted to find out if Tom knew how Dorothy felt and how he felt about living here.

When Tom and Dorothy came I informed Tom, "Your wife and I have had many talks about you, your work, and your life here in the country. What's your evaluation of living here?"

He thought for a moment and then said, "Well, to tell the truth, it hasn't turned out the way I expected. This commuting is really something. I'm so tired at night when I get home, I can't even think much less do anything. I planned to garden and go boating and do a lot of things, and I can't; I'm just too tired. It takes me all weekend to rest up so that I can go to the office on Monday." He paused and then added, "I would do anything to avoid hurting Dorothy, but you asked me to be frank. I surely would like to move back to the city. However, I'm willing to stay if it makes Dorothy happy." He turned to Dorothy and said, "You know we've never discussed it, but I assumed you really enjoy being here. Am I right?"

She shook her head no. She began, "Tom, we've had so little time to discuss anything. I didn't bring the subject up because I thought it meant so much to you to live here. You know I'd do anything to make you happy. I love you so much, I'm willing to live out here — but it gets really lonesome here. If you really want to know it, I'm homesick for the city."

"My gosh, Dorothy," Tom quickly replied, "why don't we sell out and go back home to the city where we belong?"

All she could say was, "Wouldn't it be great to get back home?" Both were happy.

Before they left, I mentioned one other matter, "Tom, I know that Dorothy loves children, and, from what she tells me, you do too. Since you can't have any children of your own, why don't you consider adopting one or two?" Tom and Dorothy looked at each other visibly shaken; tears welled up in their eyes. Tom looked at Dorothy and she looked at him. Nothing had to be said; they had made a private agreement.

After Dorothy and Tom moved back to the city, I received a card saying that they had a fine apartment but that they had to find one bigger than they had originally planned: "You see, when we saw Mike and Mitsy at the orphanage, we decided the twins were for us. They liked us too. Now we have two five-year-olds to love and care for — in addition to each other."

Later, I had a chance to see Dorothy. She informed me that she hadn't completely overcome her habit, but it rarely happened. As she said "I'm too busy to have time for self-pity and self-indulgence. Tom, Mike and Mitsy, and my church keep me busy, to say nothing of my relatives and friends."

Gerald

Gerald and Sarah Page had been living in the parish for over two years before he came to see me one evening. I hardly knew him. He and his wife came regularly to Sunday Mass but only acknowledged my greeting at the entrance to the church with a polite nod.

Gerald was a thin, shy man who found it difficult to carry on a conversation. He said, "Well, I'm not good at talking. I'm not the best educated either; I just barely made it through high school. Maybe you don't know it, but I work as a clerk in the hardware store. I've been there ever since Sarah and I moved here." After a brief pause, he continued, "I got a problem and I don't know nobody else but you to talk to." A longer pause followed. "Well, Sarah and I have been married seven years. She's a swell gal — I love her a lot, but, you see, we don't have no kids — and it's my fault. I don't know what to do but to come right out with it and say it. You see, although we've tried to have sex together a lot of times, I can't keep my organ up or have it happen the way I'm supposed to while we're making love."

He looked to see if he had shocked me or if I disapproved of the conversation. When he felt safe, he continued, "Well, it just ain't right, but the harder I try, the less I can perform. Sarah's done everythin' she can think of to help me. She's good and puts up with a lot for a long time. But, something's got to be done. Both of us want to have our own kids, but we can't if I keep this up. I figure now's the time to get help before she gets too old and won't be able to have kids." He stopped and then asked, "What'm I going to do?" My first suggestion was that he see a doctor to be sure there wasn't something physically wrong with him. He informed me that he had already seen Dr. Conley, and he said he couldn't find anything wrong.

I knew that rarely was there any physical cause for impotency and other sexual problems but that psychological factors were important. I suggested, therefore, that Gerald see the psychiatrist that lived in a neighboring town. He would not hear of it. As he said, "If you can't help me guess there's nobody to go to. I don't want to tell nobody else. It was tough enough comin' to see you." All I could do was let Gerald know I was not a professional clinician but would do what I could.

When he left, I got out my psychology books and did some studying. Later I consulted Dr. Asburn, a clinical psychologist I knew. From him I learned that *fear* is one of the potentially most important factors to consider when dealing with *relative* impotency and the inability to sustain an erection or achieve orgasm. Impotency had often been found in shy individuals and those who felt inferior around the opposite sex. It also resulted in many cases from the masturbatory activities and habits of a person. *Absolute* impotence, a physical dysfunction, rarely exists.

Armed with this information, I began immediately to explore certain possible alternatives to explain Gerald's condition. First I asked, "Gerald do you feel shy and inferior around Sarah or when you are in bed with her?"

"That could be," Gerald answered, "but that ain't all of it. I feel inferior, as you call it, when I can't do nothing . . . but I wouldn't if I didn't let me and Sarah down. She don't make me feel shy. She keeps tellin' me how great I am even when it don't happen."

I then pursued another alternative. I had never considered the possibility that Gerald masturbated. Mistakenly, I felt sure he did not. On the chance, however, that I might be wrong, I said, "Gerald, let me ask you a question. I don't mean to pry, but do you ever masturbate?" Gerald blushed and shook his head to indicate that he did. "Well, do you get an erection and have an orgasm when you masturbate?" Again, he indicated that he did.

I could hardly believe what he had just admitted. After I had elicited this admission, I continued, "But, how do you keep an erection and have an orgasm when you masturbate when you cannot perform with Sarah?"

He blushed even more, then sheepishly without looking at me he slowly stated, "I didn't think I would ever tell nobody, but I guess I gotta do it. Don't laugh at me or poke fun at me, promise?" I assured him I would not.

"Well," he began, hesitatingly, "since I was young when I put a woman's silk hanky on my face with perfume on it, I can close my eyes and have sex by myself. I still do it when Sarah can't see me."

I recalled having heard about fetishes. This was a fetish condition with Gerald. Typically, fetishism involves a centering of sexual interest on something inanimate, some body part, or a person or other animate object. It could be clothing, handkerchiefs, perfume, or countless other objects. After his admission, I asked him, "Does Sarah know about this?"

"Gosh, no," he quickly replied, "she'd laugh at me and run me out of the house for being a crazy nut.

"I can tell you, Gerald, you are not nuts, as you call it." The handkerchief and perfume are, for you, what we call 'sexual fetishes.' For reasons we don't know and may never understand, for some people certain things and, sometimes, certain people, cause a person to get sexually excited. I repeat, we don't know how they come about. To find out would take a great deal of digging and therapy by a professional psychotherapist. However, sometimes it isn't necessary to go to a therapist. If the fetish is something that does not hurt a person or hurt other people, there is no use to waste time eliminating it. Instead, it can be used. I can't see anything wrong in telling Sarah and trying using her handkerchief with perfume on it when you want to have sexual relations."

He sat silently and then he said, "I'd be too scared to tell Sarah. Do you think it's all right for her to know, and do you think you could talk to her about it?" I said I would talk with her, provided he was there at the same time. He agreed.

Two nights later, when Sarah and Gerald came to the rectory, I explained Gerald's problem to her. She was understanding and said she didn't mind if it helped. She'd help him put some perfume on a handkerchief and let him put it over his face. It was worth a try, although as she said, "It's really far out; never heard of such an arrangement, but it's okay by me, if it will do what we want."

Several days later, Gerald came to see me. He let me know that he and Sarah had sexually consummated their marriage, and sexual relations had been satisfying for both of them for the first time. Almost, as if to brag a little, he added, "Golly, Sarah went out today and bought the biggest bottle of perfume I ever saw and she also got herself some new silk handkerchiefs."

I had little else to do except aid Gerald in alleviating the guilt he felt for masturbating. However, it was agreed that I would counsel both Gerald and Sarah regarding their value system and goals, since in the future it would be necessary to include values for their children. The counseling was not begun any too soon. Within the year, Sarah had their first child. Before they left the parish five years after my first conference with Gerald, they sat each Sunday with noticeable pride in the front pew with their three children.

Margaret and Douglas

The cases of Margaret and Douglas illustrate the warped and perverted value systems that can result from negative training and attitudes toward sex and sexual activity. Often learned and accepted as true when very young, these prejudices and misconceptions are difficult to eliminate or change. No subjects occasion more resistance from clients than matters related to sexual activity; often, they refuse to discuss them or hide and distort their views. Although it may take a good deal of time and patience, it is the duty of the pastoral counselor to help individuals revise and form positive value systems. Such systems include healthy attitudes toward sex and sexual activities as God-given and potential sources of human creativity and rewarding personal and interpersonal pleasure. The attitudes of Margaret and Douglas when they came to me were so distorted and incorrect that they were, in many respects, absurd and ridiculous.

One evening I was sitting in the rectory reading. A loud, insistent knock on the door prompted me to hurry to see what was the reason. When I opened the door I was confronted with a grim-looking, slight man and a taller angry woman. I asked them to come in to my office. When they did she began immediately, "We are the Baldwins. I'm Margaret and this is my husband Douglas. I'm sure you've heard of us." I had. They were thought to be the bitterest anti-Catholic family in our community. When a census taker from the parish knocked on their door, Margaret slammed the door in his face when she learned he was from our church.

I suspected their visit had something to do with their son, Charles. I knew that he intended to marry a Catholic girl living in a neighboring parish. Margaret proved that I was correct: "Well, the worst thing that could happen to anyone in our family is happening to our son, Charles. That girl he's planning to marry has completedly turned his head. He's come from a good God-fearing, Bible-reading, Christian stock, but he called to tell us that he's going to become a Catholic. We couldn't believe it! Nothing as terrible as this has ever happened in our family. Even though we don't go to any church, we gave our children a good Christian training, especially in what was right and wrong. We thought we put the fear of God in all of them, but apparently not. The last thing we would have expected would be for one of our children to desert us and join your church." She stopped for a moment and stared angrily at me.

"Well," she continued, "the reason we're here is quite simple, Douglas and I feel someone has an obligation to let us know what Charles is getting himself into; that is, we want to know something about the Catholic church. We don't want instructions to become Catholics, perish the thought, but we'd like to have some conferences with you so that we can understand what Charles is in for." I informed them that I would be happy to arrange a series of conferences.

About a month after our conferences began, the Baldwin's youngest son came to see me. He stated, "I'd better start my instructions right away so that I can catch up with Mom and Dad. They haven't said it in so many words, but they're impressed by what you're teaching them. I'll bet they'll become Catholics. You see, we really don't have any religion and Mom's and Dad's attacks on the Catholic Church are bluffs. They were afraid of it because they didn't know anything about it." The following evening, Joseph and I began his instructions without telling his parents. However, when they came to the church to be baptized, Joseph surprised them by being there to be baptized at the same time.

In subsequent months, Margaret and Douglas became active in a number of church groups. We became close friends and often laughed about their attitudes that first night.

About a year after they were received into the church, Margaret came to me and asked if she could speak to me in private. When we entered the office, Margaret sat quietly for awhile. This was not like her. Normally, she had no problem talking. This time she did. She shook her head as if to say she did not know how to begin and what to say. Finally, she began, "father, I don't know if this is the right thing to talk about, but I need help." She paused and then continued, "Douglas and I have been married twenty-four years, but I have never once enjoyed having sexual relations. I was taught it was my duty to allow him to have intercourse, no matter how distasteful it might be for me. That has been my attitude for all these years. Even having children didn't help. In some ways, it made it worse. Now, I have become completely frigid. I dread it when Douglas asks for sexual relations, and I know he feels embarrassed and uncomfortable. He has always felt badly that I have never had a climax, but now, he feels almost ashamed to ask me to respond to him."

After a pause to catch her breath, she continued, "Well, I don't know if you remember the instructions you gave us on the Sixth Commandment and sex in general. Anyway, you presented sex in an entirely different way than Douglas and I had been taught. You saw sexual activities between a man and wife as something potentially beautiful and satisfying for both parties and a means to express physically the love each has for the other party. You went on further to say that a man or woman were permitted to experiment and find ways not only those that were necessary for the sex act but also those which would increase the pleasure for either or both parties. Well, I've never known any pleasure. What shall I do?"

First, I suggest that they should consider going to their family doctor and see if there was some physical reason for the problem. She assured me she had gone to several doctors and so had Douglas. There seemed to be nothing wrong with either of them physically. They could give her no reason for her frigidity.

I recommended that they seek the help of Dr. McCann, a clinician. They agreed, as long as I would continue counseling them, Margaret told me on her next visit. Dr. McCann and I were permitted to consult freely with each other regarding the matter. Soon all of us were convinced that the early training in sex of both Douglas and Margaret was a major factor to consider. Dr. McCann suggested that I should work with Douglas and Margaret to help them change their moral attitudes and negative approaches to sexual matters. This would involve a change in their religious and theological system so that they could develop a healthy value system with a more positive view of sex and sexual activities.

Although we met several times, it seemed we were getting nowhere; that is, until I learned some incredible facts after a private conference with Margaret. She had asked to see me without Douglas being present.

When she arrived and came to my office, she blushed and found it difficult to begin. Finally she started "Father, I don't know whether it's right or wrong to even talk about what's bothering me, but I think I know something that's at least part of my problem. I know it won't shock you, but it's embarrassing for me." She stopped, took a deep breath, and the words tumbled out of her mouth. "Father, is it wrong for me to want to see Douglas when he has an erection and is sexually excited?"

At first I thought I had not heard her correctly. I couldn't believe what I thought she said. Surely, I must have misunderstood her. I asked her to repeat her statement. She did. I had not misunderstood her. I am sure I looked astonished and amazed.

After I recovered from the shock, I said to her, "Do you mean to tell me that in twenty-four years you've never seen him when he was sexually excited? How is that possible?" "I know", she said "it may seem strange, but you see, we have never believed in undressing in front of each other. Also, we were both taught that sex was dirty but a necessary evil if one is to have children. Well, we decided before our marriage that we would never go near each other except in the dark after the lights were out and the window shades drawn. When Douglas wants intercourse, we make sure that the room is completely dark and both of us are covered by the sheet and our blankets.

I still found it hard to believe. To myself I said, "No wonder she's frigid!" She interrupted my musing

"And, now the worst thing of all, you'll have to tell me if it's wrong. I have always had the craziest desire to touch him there. Am I evil and going to hell for such thoughts?" I assured her she was not. I reminded her that I had taught both of them that men and their wives had the right to do many things which were not only necessary for the fulfillment of the act but also those things that might increase the pleasure for either of the parties. Relieved, Margaret left the office.

One week later Margaret came again to my office. She informed me that she and Douglas had been away over the weekend to a lake resort. I remember her first words. They were not said in jest but with deep feeling and meaning, "Father, even our honeymoon was nothing like it was this weekend. For the first time, I enjoyed sex, and I know Douglas was satisfied in a much more meaningful manner than he had ever experienced."

This was the beginning of a new life for the Baldwins. My role as counselor was to continue for many years. It was my responsibility to assist Douglas and Margaret in refining and expanding their value systems. With a positive and healthy attitude toward sexuality, a new theology and moral value system emerged. The God of wrath Margaret had feared as a child gave way, in her theology, to God who loved her, Douglas, their children, and all human beings. Life for both of them became a positive affirmation, rather than a negative experience. One day, Margaret said to me, "You know, I used to think I knew my Bible well. I wonder how I missed what's in the first chapter of the Bible: So God created man in his own image . . . male and female created He them. . . . And God saw everything that he had made, and, behold it was very good.' " (Gen. 1:27, 31) Unfortunately, Margaret died of cancer five years after we had terminated counseling. During those years, however, she was a joy to Douglas and her children. She was a benediction for the whole parish. Even in her last days she remained serene and calm. As she said, "I have led a full, rich life. I look forward to an even richer life in the world to come."

Mary Ellen

Mary Ellen Holland was a teacher in the local high school. She was married and had two children. Mary Ellen, her husband, and the children attended church every Sunday at 9 AM. However, I had little contact with Mary Ellen or her family until she came to me for counseling.

Mary Ellen was an attractive brunette with deep-set eyes and a sensuous mouth. She was about twenty-nine or thirty when she came one evening to the rectory. She was visibly upset. She had scarcely seated herself when she began, "Oh, Father I'm so mixed up and angry I don't know what to do." I waited until she could compose herself. Hesitatingly, she continued, "A terrible thing has happened to me. I guess I'm mentally ill, but I'm also angry at all those gossips in our school." She did not say anything for several seconds, then, "What I'm going to say is practically like I was going to confession, but I need counseling and advice at this time. Well, you know that Mark and I have been married for ten years and have two fine children. Mark is a good husband and works hard at his contracting business. My mother is a widow. She watches Charleen and Teddy when I am teaching school. Everything seemed to be going well in my life, until something happened at the beginning of this term.

"A new teacher was hired to teach biology. My reaction when I saw her for the first time was something I had never felt before. I couldn't believe it, but for the first time I found myself attracted sexually to another woman. I thought this feeling would pass, but the next time I saw her I got the same pit in my stomach that I had the first time I saw her. It didn't make sense to me. What was going on in me? Was I going crazy or something? I didn't know. I had the same feeling everytime I saw her. I kidded myself that I would avoid being around her. I was sure the feelings I got being near her were sinful and wrong. I felt I should avoid her, but I didn't seem to be able to stay away from her. That's where the anger comes in. Some of the other female teachers noticed I spent a great deal of time with or near Claudia. That's when the whispering campaign began. I was told by my best friend that one of the teachers asked, 'Just what's going on between those two, Especially with Mary Ellen? She's always hanging around Claudia?' I can assure you, Father, nothing was going on except my feeling of being attracted sexually to Claudia. I don't think she knows I'm alive. She's nice to me and all that, but I'm sure it isn't the same. I'm so mixed up, I think I will go crazy if I don't get help." She began to cry convulsively. "Can you help me?" I was more than willing to try.

When she had finished speaking I began "First of all, let me assure you that you are not crazy. Next, your feeling for Claudia should not cause you concern or feelings of anxiety and guilt. Scientific studies demonstrate that all humans are, potentially, at least, bisexual. Human beings tend, for possibly some biological reason, to be attracted to one sex in preference to the other, but the potential for being attracted to the other sex is always present. In most cases, early experiences, both pleasant and unpleasant, education, and other environmental, cultural, and religious factors determine the direction of an individual's sex drive. In most cases, it is to a heterosexual orientation. Habit, also, plays a part. After repeated sexual experiences over a period of time with either sex, a pattern of attraction is formed. As I have said, most humans become almost exclusively attracted to the opposite sex. But, there are many fine people who are exclusively or almost exclusively attracted sexually and emotionally to someone of the same sex. All must remember, however, the potential to be attracted to either sex is always present in men and women alike.

"I have counseled many men and women like yourself who were never attracted to someone of the same sex until after marriage. For many, it has caused confusion, pain, and anxiety, as it has for you. After we have finished talking, I trust it will cease to cause you concern. The main thing is for you to accept the fact that it is not unusual or abnormal to be attracted, even after a happy and fruitful marriage, to someone of the same sex. If you accept and believe what I have said, there is only one possibility of a serious problem as a result of the attraction; namely, to deny that the attraction exists. In psychology, this is called repression, and serious emotional and mental problems can result from it. The healthy and correct thing for you to do is to say to yourself, 'I'm attracted sexually to Claudia and I admit it. So what? She's an attractive woman, and I am a normal human capable of feeling as I do about her.' What you do about the attraction after this is the important thing. It becomes a matter of relative values."

After I had finished, she commented, "I understand and accept what you have told me. I will not find it difficult to handle my emotions and feelings in the future. I feel so much better now that I know I'm not crazy or evil and that it's all right for me to feel toward Claudia as I do." She paused for a moment and then concluded our conversation, "I also understand what you mean by relative values. That's no problem. I love my husband very much. If I had to choose between him or Claudia, there would be no question in my mind. It's just nice that I can feel sexually for both of them, although as far as having sexual relations, I would choose my husband, Walter. I'm even glad that it's all right to feel sexually attracted to both of them. In a way, it adds a new dimension to my life."

The next step in counseling Mary Ellen was to assist her in overcoming her anger toward her peers. Rational behavior counseling was used. Mary Ellen learned that she alone was able to determine her emotions by what she thought. The gossips could not determine her feelings. In time, she accepted the fact that they had a right to say what they wanted, even though rationally she found it regrettable. More important, she came to understand that the teachers who did the gossiping were seeing her and her relationship through subjective eyes. She learned that, without a great deal of maturity and insight, people are rarely objective about other people and what a person says, more often than not, reflects the problems, confusions, and weaknesses of the one commenting, rather than anything objective about the one being discussed. Often in counseling, I ask a client to tell me about his or her family, friends, associates, and acquaintances. The client is rarely objective, but what is said reveals a great deal about the client and the problems and outlook of the one talking.

Mary Ellen returned to her self-assured self, convinced that her life had become richer and deeper as the result of her experience.

David

David was one of the most interesting persons I had ever met. He had dedicated his life to a Christian ministry in the gay community. Although a Protestant minister, he had chosen me to be his counselor and advisor. He explained why.

"It is not only because of your knowledge of pastoral counseling but also because of your attitude toward me and those to whom I minister. What I mean is, there are many honest and well-meaning individuals who try to love every human being in a Christ-like manner no matter who or what they are. However, in reality, they only tolerate some people. This is especially true in the case of those individuals who have adopted a homosexual life-style. They say 'Believe me, I accept you as you are.' But what they really are implying is, 'I will accept you *in spite of* your homosexual inclinations.' This is not what the gay man or woman wants. He or she wants to be respected and accepted in precisely the same way that someone is respected who has decided on heterosexuality. We don't want to be treated as different, because we aren't. The plea of the gay community is the same as that of minorities all over the world: 'Don't treat us as different; treat us and respect us like you treat and respect everyone else.' Can't we learn to treat each others as

brothers and sisters whether we are black or white, Catholic or
Protestant, rich or poor, gay or straight? Like all other minorities, we are tired of condescension; we want to be accepted just
as we are and respected, regardless of our life-style. Do you see
what I mean?" I nodded that I did.

Our counseling sessions were frequent because of the many
and special problems and strains that arose because of his
unique ministry. During these meetings, I learned a great deal
about David himself and his background.

David was the oldest son of a middle-class family living in
the midwest. His mother and father were devout Christians,
and David was considered a paragon of virtue during his early
childhood and high shcool years. Everyone was convinced that
he was going to be a minister, and David had no doubt about
it, either. During high school, he dated one of the finest young
women in the church. It was assumed that he would marry her
after he finished college and had begun his theological studies.
David and Maxine both took it for granted.

However, something happened that was to change the whole
course of David's life. In his first year in college, he met Frank.
David had never been permitted to have a close male friend.
Except for dating Maxine on weekends and holidays, his father
made him stay home and study. His father was a perfectionist.
If David got a *B* instead of an *A*, he was severely reprimanded
and some of his privileges were taken away.

Something new and utterly bewildering happened inside
David. He felt a strong sexual attraction to Frank. This was the
first time such a thing had happened. In addition, it was something different than he had ever felt for Maxine. He had never
desired her sexually; he desired Frank.

He became so obsessed with the thought of Frank that he
flunked one of his major courses in college. Frank, on the other
hand, was cruel to David. He sensed David's feelings and led
him on. One day, however, he turned to David and said, "I
thought you were one of those damn queers. I wanted to find
out and I have. You are. Now go away and leave me alone!"
David was crushed. In his confusion and pain he thought
about taking his own life. He was sure he was going to hell,

and, having now been rejected by Frank, he saw no hope for himself. He thought many times, "Why not end it all?" "I would have done so," David admitted, "but I was too big a coward."

Ten years of lonely confusion followed. David's father transferred him to another school because of his poor grades. Frank went into the Marines, and David never saw him again. Along with his other studies, David was determined to learn all that he could from books about homosexuality. In his spare time, he devoured everything he could find in the library on the subject. The majority of books written by theologians categorically dismissed homosexuality as moral degeneracy or perversion, abnormal but above all "unnatural." The scientific writers disagreed; to them, it was a physical abnormality. Some held the theory of some type of hormonal imbalance; others were sure that there was a genetic reason for this "aberration." None of the theories provided a satisfactory or convincing argument for its acceptance. David remained confused. He decided to look for an answer elsewhere.

Unfortunately, he then turned to analysis, which was almost disastrous. He met a man who turned out to be a fake psychiatrist. He convinced David he was severely mentally ill and if he did not overcome his homosexual inclinations it would mean a complete mental breakdown. The only cure was a woman. He offered his wife for a substantial fee to cure David's perversion and sickness. David stopped the so-called therapy in disgust, even more confused than before. According to the experts he had consulted, he was both a moral degenerate and mentally ill.

Next, he sought the advice and assistance of a clergyman he knew. When David began to tell the man about his inclinations, an expression of horror came to the clergyman's face. All he could say was, "How terrible. You poor boy. You must pray very hard and at all time resist every thought of such sexual desires. You must put them out of your mind at all costs. I shall pray for you." With that, he dismissed David. What he did not know was that the clergyman had give him the most dangerous advice he could have received. Technically, he had been ordered to repress his feelings and emotions. This can be disastrous for one's mental health. It was almost so for David. He was on the verge of a nervous breakdown when he had to go to a hospital for a minor operation. While there, he met a doctor who had made an exhaustive study of the subject of homosexuality. For the first time David learned that homosexual drives were common and possible for human beings to feel. Kinsey and his colleagues, for example, had made an in-depth study and survey of human sexual drives. He and others in the scientific world concluded that homosexual interests and inclinations are normal and natural, not only for human beings, but all in the animal world as well. Their work led to the conclusion that all mankind is more or less bisexual, probably predisposed to sexual attraction to one sex or the other because of physical factors that were not clearly defined and understood. Finally, and critically, environmental forces and influences condition and determine actual sexual drives and behavior. For the first time, David learned that over 6 percent of the nation's adult population are sexually oriented exclusively or almost exclusively to individuals of the same sex.

David was convinced that the doctor had saved his life and his sanity. As he said, "For years I had felt nothing but agony and pain because of my homosexual inclination. I had been labeled a 'moral degenerate,' 'crazy,' a 'pervert,' a 'queer,' and many other things not fit to repeat. In reality, I had only been a normal human being who felt what any human might feel."

After he resolved the problem within himself David's life changed. As he said, "For seven years I found a peace I had not known since the day I met Frank, twelve years ago. I wasn't bothered by sex of any kind during that time. I felt I could continue to study for the ministry. After four quiet years in the seminary, I was ordained and given a small church to serve. Everything seemed to go well during my first three years there. Then something happened that was to change my whole life and ministry." He paused, then thoughtfully began again, "In our church, there are a group of laymen called the 'lay board.' The members serve not only as advisors to the pastor but control the finances as well. Once a month I met with my board to take care of financial and other matters. It was at one of these meetings as we were about to leave, Mr. Snodgrass said he had something to say that was very important and demanded our immediate attention. He said, 'I hate to bring this up, but it is in the best interest of our congregation. There is a rumor going around that our church organist, Mr. Peabody, is a homosexual. I don't know if it is true, but it is essential that we find out, because we certainly don't want that kind of person in our church, much less pay him to play the organ at our church services.' I was stunned by what he had said. I looked into the faces of the rest of the board. It was evident that most of the members agreed with him. I said nothing. I was shocked, hurt, and bewildered. It never occurred to me that a person who was homosexually oriented would not be welcome in a Christian church! I quickly dismissed the meeting and rushed to the parsonage.

"I lay awake most of the night and prayed for guidance. At one point, the beautiful prayer of Jesus in St. John's Gospel [John 10:6] came to my mind: 'And other sheep I have, which are not of this fold: them also I must bring, and they shall hear my voice; and there shall be one fold, and one shepherd.' Then and there I decided to give up the church I was serving and dedicate my ministry to working with the gay community. I hoped not only to bring Jesus' love to them but also, as a counselor, to help them avoid the living hell I had known."

I never inquired about David's personal life. He did not about mine. I do not know whether he lived as a celibate or not. I felt that it was none of my business. That was up to David, his conscience, and his God.

In the years that followed, I served not only as David's counselor but also his teacher. I helped him develop and refine his counseling skills and techniques. We discussed many things. At least three important considerations relevant to his special counseling emerged. We felt they would help his congregation in formulating their value systems and in determining their goals in life.

1. All human beings, to be healthy, must accept their emotional and sexual drives, whatever they may be. This is true of

both hetero- and homosexual feelings. Attraction to any other human, whether to the same or opposite sex, should not cause alarm or arouse feelings of guilt, inferiority, or anxiety. Accepted, rational human beings can decide what to do about emotional and sexual attractions. Repressed emotions, can cause emotional and mental illness.

2. Because one's drives and inclinations are not in accordance with the norms for a given society does not free one from developing and following standards for moral conduct according to one's conscience. Neither the homosexually oriented individual nor the heterosexually determined person is free to abandon moral standards altogether. Every individual must develop his own moral system and code of conduct. It is different for every individual, but it is incumbent on all to have such a system.

3. Every minority group, including the gay community, must accept the possibility of abuse, rejection, and prejudice. These cannot be successfully fought with useless polemics and certainly not by physical violence. The battle can be won, ultimately, only by creative contributions by the minority group to society and communicating by dialogue and other methods the differences that exist between the majority and the minority. Then, as human beings, each group can come to respect individuals in the other group as equally human, regardless of the differences in opinions, life-styles, and personal, emotional, or sexual orientations.

I missed David when he accepted the call to a larger church in the West. I remembered the prayer of the Good Shepherd that had led David to accept the challenge of his special ministry. I prayed for the day when it would not seem necessary for gay people to have separate churches because they felt rejected by other Christian groups. I prayed often another great prayer of Our Lord: "Neither pray I for these alone, but for them also which shall believe on me through their word; That they all may be one; as thou, Father, art in me, and I in thee, that they also may be one in us." (John 17:20, 21)

Part VI
Conclusion

CHAPTER 12

THE ROLE OF THE
PASTORAL COUNSELOR

THE purpose of this volume is to aid pastoral counselors in developing methods to guide individuals whose behavior is atypical. In addition to certain commentaries on atypical thinking, feeling, and acting out, case studies have been used to illustrate the application of pastoral counseling methods.

There are five important matters for a pastoral counselor to consider.

1. The chief *instrument* of the pastoral counselor is his or her own personality. Training has its place. Knowledge of atypical behavior and counseling techniques are helpful, but these are secondary to the personality of the counselor. This, in itself, makes counseling a frightening role even for those who should counsel such as pastors, priests, and rabbis, etc. There is a genuine risk in assuming the role of a counselor. A counselor is a fallible human being who makes mistakes. He is, therefore, subject to ridicule, hostility, and rejection. Nevertheless, pastoral counseling is the serious responsibility of many. It cannot be done unless one is willing to accept his own limitations and accept the possibility of minimal results and even failure.

2. Counseling is impossible unless the counselor and client can establish an empathic *rapport* and understanding relationship. It is essential that a client feels comfortable, safe, and relaxed in any counseling relationship. It is important that the counselor is able to convey to the client that he welcomes and understands the client and his pain. Such a relationship demands that the counselor is sensitive not only to what a client says but also to what he feels and what he reveals nonverbally.

A mature counselor realizes that rapport with every potential client is impossible. It may be because the counselor cannot understand the problem. It may be, on the other hand, because the counselor feels he cannot relate to the client or does not wish to enter into a counseling relationship. After meeting with the counselor, the client may feel the same way. There is nothing wrong in being honest and terminating a potential counseling relationship. In fact, at times it is essential for the welfare of the client.

3. Regardless of a counselor's skill and training and irrespective of his techniques and methods, one thing is important. The success of any counseling relationship is, for the most part, ultimately dependent on how the counselor has been able to positively influence the *thinking* of a client. In setting forth a method for counseling individuals with atypical behavior problems, many techniques and devices are used. However, regardless of approaches and techniques, only to the degree that the counselor can affect the thinking of the client, is there successful counseling. In many cases, this involves assisting clients to think more rationally. In other cases, successful counseling is influencing the client to new ways of thinking so that alternative ways of behavior can be found and maladaptive and atypical behavior is eliminated.

Periodically, a counselor should ask himself, "Am I being effective in helping the client think more positively and rationally?" If the answer is no, the counseling relationship should be terminated or the method and approach of the counselor changed. On the other hand, a counselor should not get discouraged. It is the experience of many that different and varied techniques have to be employed before the results and goals of a counseling relationship can be achieved. For this reason, it is recommended that most pastoral counselors, particularly those who are not trained as professional counselors, be eclectic in their approach to the client and counseling relationship. In many cases, simply creating an empathic understanding atmosphere in which the client feels comfortable and safe to talk is sufficient as a technique. Although it is the easiest thing to do, in many cases it is the best.

4. One of the unique roles of the pastoral counselor is to help individuals handle guilt. One should not attempt pastoral counseling until he understands the implications of irrational

and emotional guilt, in contrast to moral or rational guilt. Many individuals who display atypical behavior, particularly neurotic and other atypical feelings, have guilt as one of their major concerns. Handling moral guilt should be relatively simple for the client and counselor. The counselor needs to determine the moral value system of the client. Based upon this system, an assessment is made if any guilt exists based upon the violation of the client's moral code. For many Christians, this is not difficult. Moral or rational guilt is believed to exist only in serious matters, often defined by a systematic moral theology, when the individual knows something is wrong and does it deliberately. It follows that where there is lack of knowledge or an inability to act freely, moral guilt is lessened or does not exist at all.

Working with the irrational and emotional guilt of a client is often more difficult. In many cases, the counselor can only assist the client to see that his thinking about such guilt is irrational. In many cases, this is all the pastoral counselor can do, at least in the early stages of the counseling process. Often, another professional, such as a clinician, must be consulted by the client. The clinician enables the individual to find the underlying problem or problems that have occasioned the irrational guilt. While working with a clinician, it is possible that the pastoral counselor temporarily suspends counseling or continues to counsel the client in cooperation with the other professional. It may be that the pastoral counselor delays further counseling until the clinician had terminated his work. In all cases, however, the pastoral counselor should be available when it is in the best interest of the client to continue the counseling relationship.

5. It is the unique role of the pastoral counselor to help a client develop or alter his moral and personal value system. This involves, in many cases, an examination of the theology and religious beliefs of the client. Experience has shown that for many people, including the well-educated and trained, value systems often are weak and include many immature and inconsistent elements. Such systems are exposed as ineffective when a crisis arises in the life of an individual. Developing a

value system that is adequate under all circumstances is a life-time occupation of all humans; value systems cannot be static. They must develop, expand, and change.

It is the task of the pastoral counselor to assist in the examination, evaluation, and the reformation of a client's value system. As a counselor, it is not ethical for the counselor to impose his own theology and value system on a client. This violates his role. This is not to say, however, that as a *teacher*, a pastoral counselor may seek to influence the value system of the client, based upon the pastor's own theology and beliefs, if the client is willing. This is ethical, provided the pastor makes known his intention and the client is willing to accept the pastor's other role as a religious teacher.

Many elements go into developing a value system. Underlying all value systems is a man's or woman's theology; that is, what he or she believes about God, the Hereafter, and the purpose of human existence. In his or her role of counselor, the counselor is only indirectly interested in a client's theology and religious beliefs. There are many values that are relevant to counseling. Experience has shown that most important in dealing with all individuals but particularly with those whose behavior is atypical is the *self-concept* and *self-identity* of the client.

Experienced counselors have found that, in many cases, aside from physical causes, the loss of *personal identity* and a poor *self-concept* are basic sources and causes of many of man's problems. In many cases, an adequate self-concept never developed; in other, weak self-concepts have been undermined, at least in part, due to the dehumanizing forces at work in modern society, as well as the stresses and strains of modern living.

Regardless of the cause, it is an empirical fact that many human beings feel inadequate to handle the stresses and strains of everyday living. Dehumanized and with inadequate self-concepts, many men and women become mentally ill or seek refuge in mental illness because they cannot face or know how to handle these pressures. It is essential that all professional and functioning pastoral counselors explore with a client his self-concept and his assessment of himself as a person.

Experience has shown that a counselor can use five dimensions of the self-concept that aid in the assessment of the strengths and weaknesses of a client's self-concept. Does the client (a) lack self-esteem, self-confidence, and self-acceptance; (b) feel dependent, immature, and insecure; (c) feel estranged and lack a feeling of social worth; (d) feel sexually or physically inadequate; or (e) have a low tolerance for stress and strain? To the degree that these inadequacies exist, the self-concept is correspondingly weak and ineffective in handling anxiety and the stresses and strains caused by conflicts, frustrations, and pressures that every man and woman must face daily.

Other values, of which there are many, are secondary in pastoral counseling to a consideration of the value an individual places upon himself or herself. The Christian faith is based upon two great Commandments: to love God and to love one's neighbor as one loves himself. It follows that it is impossible to love a neighbor and love God adequately if one does not love himself. When one feels inadequate and has a poor self-concept, it is impossible to love one's self adequately. It follows that the potential to love one's neighbor and even God is reduced or, in some cases, eliminated altogether because of the absence of self-love and self-esteem. Fortunately, the Christian pastoral counselor has a theology that is significant and relevant in guiding a client to greater respect for himself as a unique person and in developing a more adequate self-concept. This is the faith and belief that can lead to a healthy self-love, self-esteem, and self-confidence. He can point out that God has made every man and woman uniquely in His own image. Further, through baptism, a human being becomes a child of God and an heir of Heaven. So sacred is the human person that St. Paul tells us God has willed that each human be a "temple of the Holy Spirit." In fact, God respected human nature so much that He took upon Himself a human nature and became man. In the words of St. Paul, "When the fullness of time was come, God sent forth his son. . . . Wherefore thou art no more a servant but a son, then an heir of God through Christ." (Gal. 4:4, 7)

BIBLIOGRAPHY

- Pastoral Counseling and Pastoral Psychology
- Abnormal Psychology
- Depression and Suicide
- Alcoholism
- Drugs
- Sex and Counseling

PASTORAL COUNSELING AND PASTORAL PSYCHOLOGY

Bordin, Edward S.: *Psychological Counseling*. New York: Appleton-Century-Crofts, 1968.

Brown, Stanley C.: *Folly or Power*. New York: Hawthorn Books, 1975.

Caplan, Ruth B.: *Helping the Helpers to Help*. New York: Seabury Press, 1972.

Clinebell, Howard J.: *Basic Types of Pastoral Counseling*. Nashville: Abingdon Press, 1966.

———: *The Mental Health Ministry of the Local Church*. Nashville: Abingdon Press, 1972.

Colston, Lowell and Hiltner, Seward: *The Context of Pastoral Counseling*. Nashville: Abingdon Press, 1961.

Draper, Edgar: *Psychiatry and Pastoral Care*. Englewood Cliffs, New Jersey: Prentice-Hall, 1965.

Faber, Heije and Vanderschoot, W.: *The Art of Pastoral Conversation*. Nashville: Abingdon Press, 1965.

Godin, Andre: *The Pastor as Counselor*. Translated by Bernard Phillips. New York: Holt, Rinehart & Winston, 1965.

Hauck, Paul A.: *Reason in Pastoral Counseling*. Philadelphia: Westminster Press, 1972.

Kemp, Charles F.: *A Pastoral Counseling Guidebook*. Nashville: Abingdon Press, 1971.

———: *Pastoral Care With The Poor*. Nashville: Abingdon Press, 1972.

Klink, Thomas W.: *Depth Perspectives in Pastoral Work*. Englewood Cliffs, New Jersey: Prentice-Hall, 1965.

Long, Louise: *Door of Hope*. Nashville: Abingdon Press, 1972.

McIntosh, Ian F.: *Pastoral Care and Pastoral Theology*. Philadelphia: Westminster Press, 1972.

179

Mikesell, William H.: *Counseling for Ministers.* North Quincy, Illinois: Christopher Books, 1961.

Nouwen, Henri J. F.: *Creative Ministry.* New York: Doubleday & Co., 1971.

Oates, Wayne E.: *New Dimensions in Pastoral Care.* Philadelphia: Fortress Press, 1970.

O'Brien, Michael J.: *An Introduction to Pastoral Counseling.* Staten Island, New York: Alba House, 1968.

Oglesby, William B.: *Referral in Pastoral Counseling.* Englewood Cliffs, New Jersey: Prentice-Hall, 1968.

Pond, Desmond: *Counseling in Religion and Psychiatry.* London: Oxford University Press, 1973.

Schaller, Lyle E.: *The Pastor and the People.* Nashville: Abingdon Press, 1973.

Simons, Joseph B. and Reidy, Jeanne: *The Human Art of Counseling.* New York: Herder & Herder, 1971.

Switzer, David K.: *The Minister as Crisis Counselor.* Nashville: Abingdon Press, 1974.

Thorton, Edward E.: *Theology and Pastoral Counseling.* Philadelphia: Fortress Press, 1964.

Vanderpool, James A.: *Person to Person: A Handbook for Pastoral Counseling.* New York: Doubleday & Co., 1977.

Vann, Gerald: *Moral Dilemmas.* New York: Doubleday & Co., 1965.

Vander Veldt, James H.: *Psychology for Counselors.* Chicago: Franciscan Herald Press, 1971.

Whitlock, Glenn E.: *Preventive Psychology and the Church.* Philadelphia: Westminster Press, 1973.

Williams, Daniel D.: *The Minister and the Cure of Souls.* New York: Harper & Row Publishers, 1961.

Wise, Carroll A.: *The Meaning of Pastoral Care.* New York: Harper & Row Publishers, 1968.

ABNORMAL PSYCHOLOGY

Balthazar, Earl E.: *The Emotionally Disturbed Mentally Retarded: A Historical and Contemporary Perspective.* Englewood Cliffs, New Jersey: Prentice-Hall, 1975.

Calhoun, Karen S.: *Innovative Treatment Methods in Psychopathology.* New York: John Wiley & Sons, 1974.

Coleman, James C.: *Abnormal Psychology and Modern Life,* 3rd ed. Chicago: Scott, Foresman & Co., 1964.

English, Oliver S.: *Emotional Problems of Living.* New York: W. W. Norton & Co., 1972.

Finkel, Norma J.: *Mental Illness and Health.* New York: Macmillan Publishing Co., 1976.

Kisker, George W.: *The Disorganized Personality*. New York: McGraw-Hill Book Co., 1972.

Kobler, Frank J.: *Casebook in Psychotherapy*. Staten Island, New York: Alba House, 1964.

Lazarus, Richard J.: *Patterns of Adjustment*. New York: McGraw-Hill Book Co., 1976.

Maher, Brendan A.: *Contemporary Abnormal Psychology*. Selected readings. New York: Penguin Books, 1973.

Millon, Theodore: *Abnormal Behavior and Personality*. Philadelphia: W. B. Saunders Co., 1974.

Mowrer, Orval J.: *The Crisis in Psychiatry and Religion*. Princeton, New Jersey: Van Nostrand Reinhold Co., 1961.

Perrucci, Robert: *Circle of Sadness*. Englewood Cliffs, New Jersey: Prentice-Hall, 1974.

Sarason, Irwin G.: *Abnormal Psychology: The Problem of Maladaptive Behavior*. Englewood Cliffs, New Jersey: Prentice-Hall, 1976.

DEPRESSION AND SUICIDE

Alvarez, Alfred: *The Savage God*. New York: Random House, 1972.

Choron, Jacques: *Suicide*. New York: Charles Scribner's Sons, 1972.

Farber, Maurice L.: *Theory of Suicide*. New York: Funk & Wagnalls Co., 1968.

Grollman, Earl A.: *Suicide Prevention, Intervention, Postvention*. Boston: Beacon Press, 1971.

Hafen, Brent Q.: *Self-Destructive Behavior*. Minneapolis: Burgess Publishing Co., 1972.

Hendin, Herbert: *The Age of Sensation*. New York: W. W. Norton & Co., 1975.

Jacobs, Jerry: *Adolescent Suicide*. New York: John Wiley & Sons, 1971.

Lester, Gene and Lester, David: *Suicide: the Gamble with Death*. Englewood Cliffs, New Jersey: Prentice-Hall, 1971.

McCulloch, Wallace: *Suicidal Behavior*. New York: Pergamon Press, 1972.

Mannes, Marya: *Last Rights*. New York: William Morrow & Co., 1974.

Pederson, Duane: *Going Sideways: Hope, Love, Life Versus Suicide*. New York: Hawthorn Books, 1974.

Prentice, Ann E.: *Suicide: A Selective Bibliography of Over 2200 Items*. Metuchen, New Jersey: Scarecrow Press, 1974.

Pretzel, Paul W.: *Understanding and Counseling the Suicidal Person*. Nashville: Abingdon Press, 1972.

Stone, Howard W.: *Suicide and Grief*. Philadelphia: Fortress Press, 1972.

Weisman, Avery D.: *The Realization of Death*. New York: Jason Aronson, 1974.

ALCOHOLISM

Al-Anon: *Living with an Alcoholic*. New York: Al-Anon Family Group Headquarters, 1976.

Alateen: *Hope for Children of Alcoholics*. New York: Al-Anon Family Group Headquarters, 1973.

Alcoholics Anonymous, 16th ed. New York: Alcoholics Anonymous Publishers, 1954.

Burgess, Louise B.: *Alcohol and Your Health*. North Hollywood, California: Charles Publishing Co., 1973.

Burns, John: *The Answer to Addiction*. New York: Harper & Row Publishers, 1975.

Cahn, Sidney: *The Treatment of Alcoholics*. London: Oxford Press, 1970.

Clinebell, Howard J., Jr. *Understanding and Counseling the Alcoholic Thru Religion and Psychology*. Nashville: Abington Press, 1968.

Coudert, Jo: *The Alcoholic in Your Life*. Chicago: Stein Publishing House, 1972.

Fort, Joel: *Alcoholism: Our Biggest Drug Problem*. New York: McGraw-Hill Book Co., 1973.

Gammage, Allen Z.: *Alcoholism, Skid Row and the Police*. Spingfield, Illinois: Charles C Thomas, Publisher, 1972.

Johnson, Vernon E.: *I'll Quit Tomorrow*. New York: Harper & Row Publishers, 1973.

Larkin, E. J.: *The Treatment of Alcoholism: Theory, Practice and Evaluation*. Ontario, Canada: Addiction Research Foundation, 1974.

McLlwan, William A.: *Farewell to Alcohol*. New York: Random House, 1972.

Madsen, William: *The American Alcoholic*. Springfield, Illinois: Charles C Thomas, Publisher, 1974.

Mann, Marty: *New Primer on Alcoholism*. New York: Holt, Rinehart & Winston, 1958.

Moore, Guy P.: *Management and Approach to Alcoholism*. San Mateo, California: Jones Pub., 1975.

Moses, Donald A.: *Are You Driving Your Children to Drink?* Princeton, New Jersey: Van Nostrand Reinhold Co., 1975.

Rutgers University: *A Cross Cultural Study of Drinking*. New Brunswick, New Jersey: Rutgers University Press, 1975.

Silverstein, Alvin: *Alcoholism*. Philadelphia: J. B. Lippincott Co., 1975.

Steiner, Claude: *Games Alcoholics Play*. New York: Grove Press, 1971.

Stewart, David A.: *Thirst For Freedom*. Center City, Minnesota: Hazeldon, 1960.

———: *The Adventure of Sobriety*. East Lansing, Michigan State University Press, 1976.

Tracy, Don: *What You Should Know About Alcoholism*. New York: Dodd, Mead & Co., 1975.

Vanderpool, James A.: Alcoholism and the self-concept. *Quarterly Journal of Studies on Alcohol*, Vol. 30, No. 1, pp. 59-77, March, 1969.

Willis, James H.: *Addiction: Drugs and Alcohol Re-Examined.* Belmont, California: Pitman Publishing Corp., 1973

DRUGS

Alexander, Clifton: *How to Kick the Habit.* New York: Frederick Fell, 1972.

Altonsi, Phillip and Pesnoit, Patrick: *Satan's Needle.* New York: William Morrow & Co., 1972.

Blum, Richard H.: *The Dream Sellers.* San Francisco: Jossey-Bass, 1972.

Brecher, Edward M.: *Licit and Illicit Drugs.* Boston: Little, Brown & Co., 1972.

Brown, Clinton C. and Savage, Charles: *The Drug Abuse Controversy.* Baltimore: National Educational Consultants, 1971.

Cassel, Russell N.: *Drug Abuse Education.* North Quincy, Illinois: Christopher Books, 1971.

The Child Study Association of America: *You, Your Child and Drugs.* New York: The Child Study Press, 1971.

Cooley, Leland F.; *Pre-Meditated Murder.* Radnor, Pennsylvania: Chilton Book Co., 1971.

Dealing With Drug Abuse. A report to the Ford Foundation. New York: Praeger Publishers, 1973.

Densen-Gerber, Judianne and Baden, Trissa A.: *Drugs, Sex, Parents and You.* Philadelphia: J. B. Lippincott Co., 1972.

Edwards, Carl N.: *Drug Dependence; Social Regulation and Treatment Alternatives.* New York: Jason Aronson, 1974.

Einstein, Stanley: *Beyond Drugs.* Elmsford, New Jersey: Pergamon Press, 1975.

Ferguson, Robert W.: *Drug Abuse Control.* Boston: Holbrook Press, 1975.

Finlator, John: *The Drugged Nation: A Narc's Story.* New York: Simon & Schuster, 1975.

Geller, Allen and Boas, Maxwell: *The Drug Beat: A Complete Survey of the History, Distribution, Uses and Abuses of Marijuana, LSD and the Amphetamines.* Chicago: Henry Regnery Co., 1969.

Goshen, Charles: *Drinks, Drugs, and Do-Gooders.* New York: The Free Press, 1973.

Halberstom, Michael: *The Pills in Your Life.* New York: Grosset & Dunlap, 1972.

Harper, Frederick D.: *Alcohol Abuse and Black America.* Alexandria, Virginia: Douglass Publishers, 1976.

Hyde, Margaret O.: *Mind Drugs.* New York: McGraw-Hill Book Co., 1972.

Kastl, Albert J. and Kastl, Lena: *Journey Back: Escaping the Drug Trap.*

Chicago: Nelson-Hall Co., 1975.

Kiev, Ari: *The Drug Epidemic.* New York: The Free Press, 1975.

Lennard, Henry L. et al.: *Mystification and Drug Misuse.* San Francisco: Jossey-Bass, 1971.

Marin, Peter and Cohen, Allan Y.: *Understanding Drug Use: An Adult's ·Guide to Drugs and the Young.* New York: Harper & Row Publishers, 1971.

Martindale, Don A.: *The Social Dimensions of Mental Illness, Alcoholism, and Drug Dependence.* Westport, Connecticut: Greenwood Press, 1971.

Morse, Tom: *When the Music Stops.* Old Tappan, New Jersey: Fleming H. Revell Co., 1971.

Ray, Oakley S.: *Drugs, Society and Human Behavior.* St. Louis: C. V. Mosby Co., 1972.

Rice, Julius: *Ups and Downs.* New York: Macmillan Publishing Co., 1972.

Rosenthal, Mitchell S. and Mothner, Ira: *Drugs, Parents and Children: The Three-Way Connection.* Boston: Houghton Mifflin Co., 1972.

Smith, David E.: *Uppers and Downers.* Englewood Cliffs, New Jersey: Prentice-Hall, 1973.

Sorenson, Andrew A.: *Confronting Drug Abuse.* Philadelphia: Pilgrim Press, 1972.

Strauss, Nathan III: *Addicts and Drug Abusers: Current Approaches to the Problem.* New York: Twayne Publications, Division of G. K. Hall, 1971.

Susan, Jackwell: *Drug Use and Social Policy.* New York: AMS Press, 1972.

Way, Walter L.: *The Drug Scene: Help or Hang Up.* Englewood Cliffs, New Jersey: Prentice-Hall, 1970.

Willis, James H. P. *Addicts: Drugs and Alcohol Re-Examined.* Belmont, California: Pitman Publishing Corp., 1973.

SEX AND COUNSELING

Beach, F. A. (Ed.): *Sex and Behavior.* New York: John Wiley & Sons, 1965.

Blenkinsopp, Joseph: *Sexuality and the Christian Tradition.* Dayton, Ohio: Pflaum Press, 1969.

Churchill, W.: *Homosexual Behavior Among Males.* New York: Hawthorn Books, 1967.

Daly, Mary: *The Church and the Second Sex.* New York: Harper & Row Publishers, 1968.

Doely, Sarah Bentley (Ed.): *Women's Liberation and the Church.* New York: Association Press, 1970.

Francoeur, Robert T.: *Eve's New Rib.* New York: Harcourt Brace Jovanovich, 1972.

Janeway, Elizabeth: *Man's World, Woman's Place: A Study in Social Mythology.* New York: William Morrow & Co., 1971.

Karlen, Arno: *Sexuality and Homosexuality: A New View.* New York: W. W. Norton & Co., 1971.

Kinsey, A. C., Pomeroy, W. B., and Martin, C. E.: *Sexual Behavior in the Human Male.* Philadelphia: W. B. Saunders Co., 1948.

Kinsey, A. C., Pomeroy, W. B., Martin, C. E. and Gebhard, P. H.: *Sexual Behavior in the Human Female.* Philadelphia: W. B. Saunders Co., 1953.

Mace, David R.: *The Christian Response to the Sexual Revolution.* Nashville: Abingdon Press, 1970.

Masters, William H. and Johnson, Virginia E.: *Human Sexual Inadequacy.* Boston: Little, Brown & Co., 1970.

McNeill, John: *Church and the Homosexual.* Mission, Kansas: Sheed Andrews and McMeel, 1976.

Parker, W.: *Homosexuality: A Selective Bibliography of Over 3000 Items.* Metuchen, New Jersey: Scarecrow Press, 1971.

Roy, Rustum and Roy Della: *Honest Sex.* New York: New American Library, 1972.

Stroup, Herbert W., Jr., and Wood, Norma S.: *Sexuality and the Counseling Pastor.* Philadelphia: Fortress Press, 1974.

Thielicke, Helmut: *The Ethics of Sex.* Translated by John W. Doberstein. New York: Harper & Row Publishers, 1964.

Tripp, C. A.: *The Homosexual Matrix.* New York: McGraw-Hill Book Co., 1975.

Weinberg, G. H.: *Society and the Healthy Homosexual.* New York: St. Martin's Press, 1972.

Weinberg, M. S. and Bell, A. P.: *Homosexuality: An Annotated Bibliography.* New York: Harper & Row Publishers, 1972.

Weinberg, M. S. and Williams, C. J.: *Male Homosexuals.* New York: Oxford University Press, 1974.

Wood, Frederic C., Jr.: *Sex and the New Morality.* New York: Association Press, 1968.

Wysor, B.: *The Lesbian Myth.* New York: Random House, 1974.

INDEX